FULL STORY EDITION

STICKS
AND STONES

Poetry
and Prose

CHELSEA DEVRIES

Sticks & Stones
Poetry and Prose: The Full Story

Scripture taken from *Holy Bible,* New Living Translation. Copyright 1996, 2004, 2007 by Tyndale House Foundation. Used by permission of Tyndale House Publishers, Inc., Carol Stream, Illinois 60188. All rights reserved.

Scripture taken from The Message. Copyright 1993, 1994, 1995, 1996, 2000, 2001, 2002. Used by permission of NavPress Publishing Group.

Author Photo: Lulu Seldon, luluseldonphotography.com
ISBN: 978-0-578-95865-1
One Girl Revolution

STICKS
AND STONES

ADVANCE PRAISE FOR *STICKS & STONES*

"Chelsea's collection takes you on a raw and honest journey into the unknown. Her writing is vulnerable yet powerful, allowing you to realize that you have strength, even when you feel your weakest. This book shows the complexity of life and love and all things in between. Though trauma exists, you don't have to let it consume you. Chelsea is a warrior, and after reading this, you'll feel like one too. 'Sticks and stones may break your bones' but words will help to heal you."
— **Venetia, @venxtiapoetry & Self-Care Artist**

Chelsea is such a sweet and beautiful soul and that definitely comes across in her poems. This book uses poetry to tell the story of her experiences working in a toxic work environment and how she found and lost a love that left her broken and with a desire to heal and rebuild. Chelsea is very transparent in this book and I loved how she held nothing back. It is obvious that she's passionate about growing as a person through her faith, passions, and journey to self love. This book was such a lovely introduction into the world of poetry and definitely left me wanting to read more.
— **@pageturnrave on Instagram**

With her love of the Lord and herself, Chelsea shows readers that it's through such experiences, however emotionally draining they may be, that we learn & grow. I have respect for such talent for poetry to help one get through such hurt. Such a lovely, deep form of catharsis this collection of poetry & prose is.
— **@books.bargains.n.brands on Instagram**

Chelsea has written everything without any hesitation. She mentions everything about mental breakdown and sexual assault. It is very courageous

to share her story and must be appreciated. Not everyone has the guts to do that.
— **Indian Reviewer on Instagram (@officialtanishq)**

This book is really beautiful. Much respect and Power to Chelsea. This book takes you on a raw and honest journey into the unknown. Her writing is vulnerable yet powerful, allowing you to realize that you have strength, even when you feel your weakest. Her journey of suffering from toxicity, sexual assault, heartbreak to being a happy and powerful soul is inspiring.
— **Shenzoo (@twins.reading.books)**

Chelsea is a warrior, and after reading this, you'll feel like one too. 'Sticks and stones may break your bones' but words will help to heal you." I wish I could hug you and thank you for inspiring so many girls/women out there who had gone through all this.
— **Shanaya (@twins.reading.books)**

This book is a personal account of a woman's pain. The author did not hold back in sharing her story. I love the fact that the stories are real and many women can relate to them. The title is quite fitting for the stories told in this collection. This book reminded me that we may have similar stories but our journeys are not the same. Every story here is testimony that healing is an ongoing process and we have the power to share our pain through poetry as we heal.
— **Stacie Ann Green-Taylor , Author of *I Found My Heart***

The realities of life and emotional turbulence shared in honest, and gut wrenching detail through prose and poetry. A book to which many readers will relate. Expressing the ultimate lows to which life can cause us to crumble, any how we can survive, but must never cease fighting the battle that will provide us with a semblance of happiness.
— **Amazon Reviewer**

Just wow! This book resonated so much and is so relatable. While everyone usually shies away from truly writing their experiences from a love that was not reciprocated Chelsea did an amazing job at capturing how I believe we all once felt in our lives. From being smitten to being ignored, from being silenced to finding your voice, from being in a dark place to finding some light. We can all find at least one or more pages/poems where we can sit there and reread cause it was like Chelsea was reading your minds of how we once felt. Praise for Sticks + Stones.
— **Goodreads Reviewer**

It is an exquisite piece of an art, where it helps you enhance all kind of emotions that one might experience in their life.
Beauty lies in simplicity and that's what the author has done with her work. The author definitely poured her heart out. The poems deliver the message of healing through the pain. You grow through what you go through.
I found myself smiling, laughing, and tearing up as I read. So beautifully written. I felt every word! The majority of the poems were pleasant and relatable. So many of these poems felt like a punch in the chest, they took my breath away.
Highly recommended!
— **Indian Reviewer on Instagram (@read_by_heart)**

There is heart and emotions behind this book. As a writer, as a human being, we bear our souls when it comes to our work and life's experiences. We want to be seen, heard, and most importantly, we need to feel like we exist. This book did not fall on deaf ears, or rather it didn't pass me without noticing. But I do know this spoke to me. It brought back memories of past love, regret, self— denial of wanting what may have been out of my reach in my youth to begin with... Even friendships lost. All are a part of life. My life. Her life. And I understand hers a bit better now. ~ppreciate that.
— ~. ~zon **Reviewer**

Sticks and Stones is a torturous and twisted read and the formaldehyde perfume intrigues me.
— **Barnes and Noble Reviewer**

A volume of poetry and prose focuses on a toxic work environment. In the preface, DeVries lays bare a litany of wrongdoings she's suffered. The intent of sharing these harrowing experiences is admirable. In addition, the author's similes and metaphors are often clever or heartfelt. A sincere and timely collection.
— **Kirkus**

The author has shown courage by writing this poetry book, even after having an unpleasant experience. Every poem defines the feelings of the author that how, despite the difficulties of life, she has stood up all over again. Instead of falling apart. She gathered all the courage and took action to rebuild herself. This book is a self help/inspiration expressed through poetry. The abstract poetry will make you feel emotional and happy at the same time. It'll encourage you towards self— love. The writing style is lucid. Every poem conveys the message clearly.
— **Avinash Meshram, Author of** *Her Perfect Man!*

In this book, poetry serves as an instrument to tell a story about finding the courage to stand up against oppression and the strength to overcome internal struggles. What I like most is the author's authenticity. The way the author bled all over these pieces is evident in her tone and choice of words. She made the poems very personalized and tailored to her own experiences, creating a coherent story throughout the collection. I commend the author for the courage to deliver an honest story that will empower many others. I think poetry enthusiasts who adore poems about love and empowerment will find this book a pleasurable read.
— **OnlineBookClub.org Reviewer**

Honest. Powerful truths and personal accounts. I was pleased with the authors choice of words. I will say that this work is empowering, for anyone that has felt less than. This is your story as well.

— S.S. Baker, Author of *Cerebral Fossil*

NOTE TO READERS

Dear Reader

At the young age of 14, I wrote a poem that I never planned on showing anyone. I remember sitting in English class in high school and the words just poured out of me. For the life of me, I don't even know what we were studying but that poem would actually serve as my first publishing credit overall because it later was accepted in a student anthology.

That poem was called LOVE ME FOR ME.

I published this collection of poetry wanting to share my story in a poetic way but also come out with truths I never shared with anyone.

I pray this collection resonates with you. It feeds your soul, it triggers you to do what you need to become your highest self and the best version of you.

Most of all, I hope it greets you in the midst of my darkness and better paints the full picture for you that time, love, and setting proper boundaries really does heal all wounds.

Lastly, I ask that you practice proper self-care before, during, and after reading this collection.

Thank you,

Chelsea DeVries

PREFACE

I was scheduled to put out a novel before this collection of poetry but what I've been through in the last year resulted in this collection. It is called *Sticks & Stones* due to the fact that what I went through was a double trauma resulting from spending 10 months working at a place that felt like sandpaper on my skin.

Prior to that, I've been through experiences that I feel like made me grow up much too fast. I was sexually assaulted twice before I was 13 by two different men, I was diagnosed with a thyroid disorder while I was a junior in college only to finally get an appointment with a medical doctor who ended up nearly killing me and then subsequently covering up her medical negligence, and making it look like I had freaking bird flu so I couldn't even sue her, and she still practices medicine in my city.

I have been bullied, outcasted, made to feel ostracized by my peers every year from kindergarten until I graduated college.

After suffering that traumatic near death experience, I realized I had mental illness while watching the movie Perks of Being a Wallflower, and I wrote a poem originally called Suicide Note because I just didn't want to be any more weirder than people already made me feel. I struggled once again with this idea that I shouldn't even try living the way I am because people don't typically choose to stick around when I show them the demons inside me.

Even more tragic was I nearly failed out of college due to that doctor's negligence and graduated by the goddamn skin on my teeth only to not even be included in the commencement program.

Then, I graduated college and ended up finally finding a full-time job that illusively looked like a dream.

Until that dream became a nightmare that ended up resembling a real-life depiction of Taylor Swift's The Man.

I was emotionally abused by the boss's wife.

I was sexually harassed by a coworker and my boss.

I watched day after day as the guys I worked alongside were talked about, demeaned, belittled, and kept in a poverty mindset by management and family.

I ended up falling in love with a guy that worked there without ever telling him, but when I finally thought it was safe to tell him, he blocked me and ignored my text messages, and I was left to pick up the pieces of my sad little heart not understanding how you could think so highly of someone who ends up leaving you in the end.

One image has always stuck with me no matter what I've gone through in life and I believe it is a great image to begin this collection with as well as to go back to after you read most of these poems and passages.

In John 8, we find the story of the woman caught in adultery and how Jesus reacted to her and the religious people of his day. She was thrown into the middle of the street and all the religious men were prepared to stone her when Jesus approaches:

"Teacher," they said to Jesus, "this woman was caught in the act of adultery. [5] The law of Moses says to stone her. What do you say?"

[6] They were trying to trap him into saying something they could use against him, but Jesus stooped down and wrote in the dust with his finger. [7] They kept demanding an answer, so he stood up again and said, "All right, but let the one who has never sinned throw the first stone!" [8] Then he stooped down again and wrote in the dust.

[9] When the accusers heard this, they slipped away one by one, beginning with the oldest, until only Jesus was left in the middle of the crowd with the woman. [10] Then Jesus stood up again and said to the woman, "Where are your accusers? Didn't even one of them condemn you?"

[11] "No, Lord," she said.

And Jesus said, "Neither do I. Go and sin no more," (NLT).

Society and the people in it are always so quick to want to throw stones at you without realizing that not one of us is without blame, shame, or guilt due to something we've done, said, or that was done to us.

It's something I always try to do in my life is be merciful despite the sticks and stones people throw at me.

Yet, this last year taught me that sometimes being merciful doesn't mean staying quiet or playing nice.

It means reaching out, speaking up, yelling "STOP!" when someone's actions, words, or body language seem to come against you and make you feel uncomfortable, inferior, or inadequate.

As you can clearly see, a lot of sticks and stones have been thrown at me but I've decided to use them to rebuild me and all the people who have ever felt the same.

I hope these poems give you the courage to know the difference between when to be merciful and knowing when to be merciless, and when to walk away from people who always make it a point to focus on your mistakes.

Love always,
Chelsea xoxo

DEDICATION

This book is dedicated to anyone who has ever worked in a toxic work environment, who has had to endure any form of abuse.

If you or someone you know is currently working in a place where you are being harassed or abused, please feel free to reach out to **betterbrave.org** as they are a non-profit organization dedicated to helping employees become braver and speak out about unfair treatment within the workplace.

And those who were seen dancing were thought to be insane by those who could not hear the music.
—Friedrich Nietzsche

This is dedicated to anyone who has been told they are "too" anything and have always felt like they had to stand on the outside of life's lines: They may try to water down your colors but you keep painting the canvas with acrylic vibrancy. This world was meant to be seen in color vision.

PART 1

Sticks

If the wicked are shown grace, they don't seem to get it. In the land of right living, they persist in wrong living, blind to the splendor of God.
-Isaiah 26:10, The MSG

Everything in the world is about to be wrapped up, so take nothing for granted. Stay wide-awake in prayer. Most of all, love each other as if your life depended on it. Love makes up for practically anything. Be quick to give a meal to the hungry, a bed to the homeless— cheerfully. Be generous with the different things God gave you, passing them around so all get in on it: if words, let it be God's words; if help, let it be God's hearty help. That way, God's bright presence will be evident in everything through Jesus, and he'll get all the credit as the One mighty in everything— encores to the end of time. Oh, yes!
-1 Peter 4:7-11, The MSG

Sticks:
a thin piece of wood that has fallen or been cut from a tree.

Example: **She gathered the sticks they threw at her together and tossed them in the fire
To create a collection of poetry.**

I've been misunderstood
More times than most can
Knock on wood
But
I am lucky to be alive
Ready to soar
Willing to thrive.

Life is but a prize
For those who know
The struggle
To survive.
Love Me For Me
Love me for who I have become,
Not for who I was.
Love me for my natural beauty,
Not for my plastered beauty.
Love me not for my smile,
But the love that shines through it.
Love me not for my apparel,
But for my sense of humor.
Love me not for my laugh,
But for the kindness that shines through it.
All I ask of you is that:
You love me for me.

DESERT MIRAGE

I don't know how to feel
today
my mind has gone
away
because my heart has broken
in two.

Here I stand
glass pieces of my heart
surround me
holding out my wrists
they cut me.

You stand above me
watch me bleed
a smirk plays
upon your face
as you tell me I've been replaced.

You never loved me
I was just a toy
watch me go
Girl leaves boy.

It's sad
I'm still not enough.
Sandpaper truth,
jagged and rough.

I wanted so much
to be all you need
but you would rather
leave me to bleed.

I will rise
I will not die
I will live
to make you wish
I wasn't alive.

OGRES AND HUNCHBACKS

Growing up,
I was mesmerized by Esmeralda.

I never understood why
Until recently.

Sure, she was pretty and seductive
But that is most woman's charm.

She was a gypsy
Able to run free.

Turns out
After all the hours
I've turned into
Quasimodo
In his bell tower.

Hoping and praying for one day
Where I don't have to hide my face
Or be ashamed
Of how out of place
I am.
Too many Frollos
Have spoken for me.
Told me I'm safer
Locked in
Cooped up.

You should hide.
After all,
You are nothing
Like them.

But if Shrek
Could find
A talking donkey
To befriend
And an ogre
To wed.

All I must do
Is peel back
The layers of my onion
Inside.

Step into the light.
Be unashamed.
Let people stare.
I no longer refuse to hide.

I will wear
The colorful threads
Purple in my hair
Wear Etnies
Although I don't skate.

In order to make it
In this life,
You have to let people in
You need to receive love
In order to thrive.

THE ENTERTAINER

Joplin had the melody
Let me see if I can bring
The lyrics.

I always liked being on the stage.

On the stage,
Everyone was looking at me in awe
Instead of fright

Nobody gave me sympathy eyes
And I heard no whispers of,

"Is she all right?"

The name of the game
Is to be a vessel
An outlet
For the stage lights to beam through

Make 'em laugh, Make 'em cry
But whatever you do
Don't make 'em throw tomatoes
And boo you.

I grew up wanting to sing
And dance
Like Britney Spears.

But just like making it
in the mickey mouse club
You could say
I missed my chance.

I did everything
To convince
My parents that theater
Was where my heart soared

And the world could hear my voice
In a song

Then, came poetry
Fast and quick
Something that stuck to my ribs
Equivalent of that line from Slim
About Mom's spaghetti

I thought I could be the female Eminem
Or the girl version of Lil Wayne
But urban poetry is the song of
the struggle, the hustle, the game.

You provide the imagery
The metaphors
The lines
Over a bumping bass beat.

Not so much so people
Can move their feet
But instead
Not be defeated by the monsters

We hide under our beds and in our closets.

Societies twisted lies
That the rich get richer
The poor stay poor.

Give glory to the right relic
It will open so many doors.

I can't ignore
That like never before
I still crave the lights,
The cameras,
The music,
The stage.

God gave me this mission
He asked me to entertain you.

He doesn't want you to remain blue.
Only be mesmerized by the show,
The music,
The green and blue lights.

If nobody clapped at the end of your set,
Would you still stand under the spotlight?

DIFFERENT DRUM

I didn't belong in ballet
Although I was good at tap

So I split from dance class.

I hated the idea of PE in the 6th grade
So I joined the band
Demanded they let me clash some cymbals,
Pound the bass drum,
Tinkle a melody across the bells
Drumroll along the top of the snare.

Until they said I had to carry
The drum on my back for all parades.

I marched on;
our rhythms were off.

Needing a place to belong
A friend opened a magazine
Showed me a two page spread
Of this little five foot guy
Defying gravity overtop of it.
I googled his name
It rhymed with heckler.

I sent out for an autographed poster
From him and got one back.

Chelsea,
Thank you for the support.
It read.

My life only
Got better
When I followed the
Melody
Of the music
In my soul
Calling me home

To a dirty and dark
Mostly hot
Concrete jungle

Where rap and grunge rock
Meet
The soundtrack
Of urethane wheels
On concrete.

Each time I visit
I see a mix of skin colors,
And faces,
Music tastes, styles,
All together in one place.

Rooting for one guy or girl
To win first place
But instead of competitors
I am greeted
With a sense of comradery

And friendship.

When we go one,
We go all
Type of deal.

And it's here
Where the energy is unmatched
My soul feels at peace.
And I belong.

No matter the distance
Whether together or apart

One thing is sure
And true about me.

Skateboarding will
forever
Kickflip My Heart.

CAFFEINE WITHDRAWAL

I met a tall
cup of hot
java
at the library.

Approaching me
he opened my
eyes
to God's
plan in disguise.

Day three
he spoke to me.

Day seven
I hit heaven
open mouthed
stare
I received.

I thank you
Coffee
for opening
my eyes
but you've
left Leo;
unless you
facebook

our story
has ended.

You wanted me
I wanted you
burner burned out;
electrocuted fuse.

I lost my mind
in your kind of brew.

I'll reconsider my
drink of choice
if you choose
the right sweetener.

3 sweet lines;
2 creamy pursuits.

Too strong;
too bitter,
unstable you.

Now you see why
I've exiled coffee.

At the sight of him
I became too jittery.

Now, I only
drink tea.

PERKS OF BEING A WALLFLOWER

I'm just a girl
Really strong
like petals on a flower

I wilt.

Underneath this smile
No one comes to water me
or bring me sunshine

All I can see
are dark clouds
ominous yet sad.
Hope deflated
like helium in a balloon.

I'm just a girl
who wants that boy
with the sensitive side
to tell her she's beautiful
right before he kisses her.
I just want one person
to have their life
changed by the words
I write
on this page…

In that moment,
I'll know I'm not alone.

Though the truth
is hard to swallow
when it's choking you

You know what else
is hard to swallow?

Life.
People leave without explanation.
Good people die too young.
Bad people get all the glory,
invites and friends.

If you don't know
what you want to do in life,
you're labeled a loser.
If you've never been kissed,
you're labeled a prude.

I'm just a girl
pretty like a flower
society has pushed me
up against
a wall.

Does that make me a wallflower?
Am I nobody for observing life instead of participating?

I'm a strong wallflower
but I wilt
sometimes I need water
a little rain

lots of sunshine.
Mostly
just love
to know someone
anyone
cares.

I'm just a girl
with a beautiful heart and smile
who doesn't believe in herself.

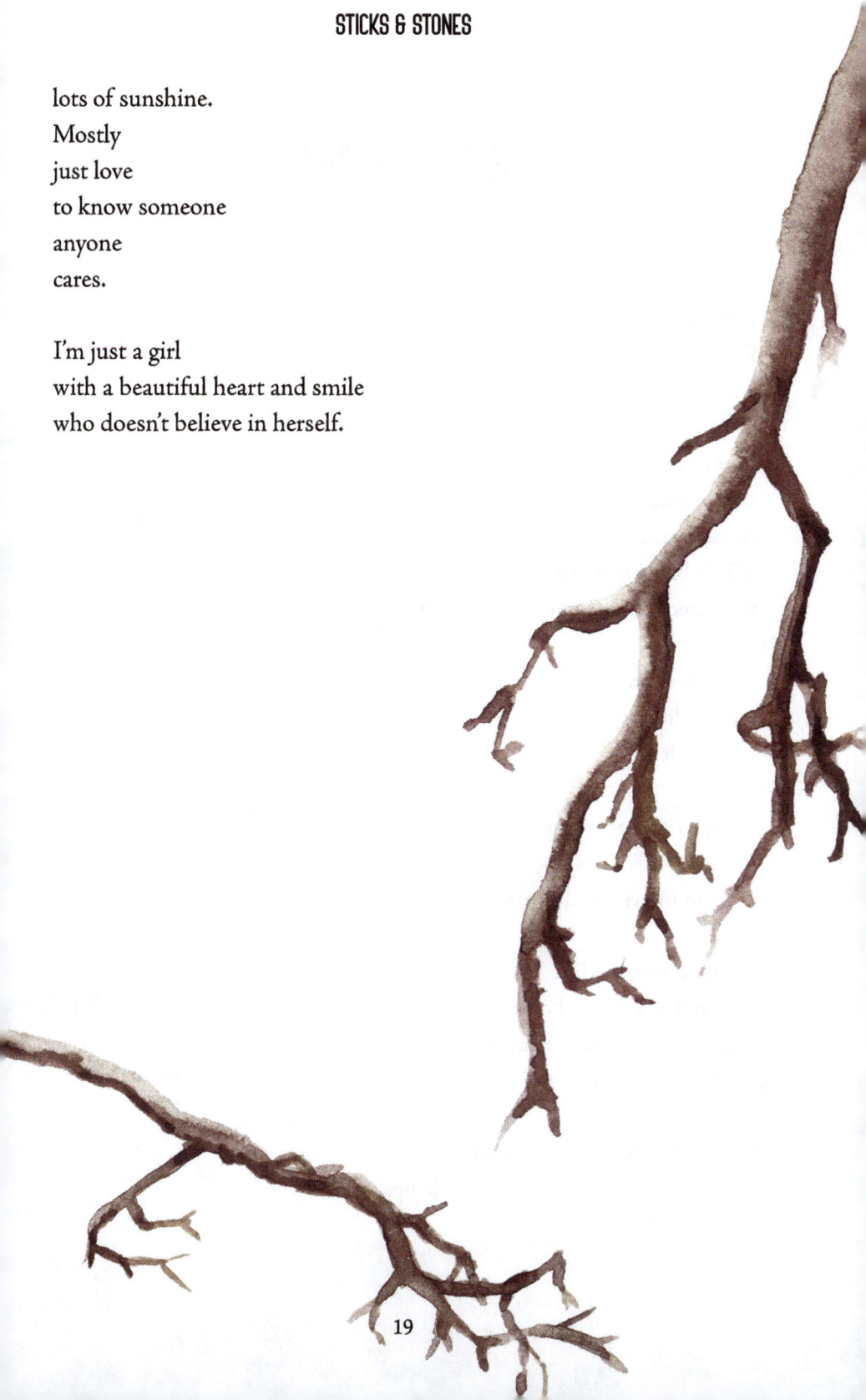

HAPPY MEDIUM

What's The Difference
Between
Keeping Quiet
and Suffering in Silence?

It's one breath between
swallowing
A thousand pins
While being stabbed
Repeatedly in the gut

Trouble slams the door
repeatedly
while I sleep

There's nothing worse
for me
than an interrupted dream

I crave it like Godiva
Covered in whipped cream
A chocolate covered strawberry
Dripping in melted desire

I think I'm just hungry for love
I have no appetite for casual hook-ups
kissing and telling

Having my freak
out in the streets
no matter how good I turn out and up
in the sheets

How long until I can finally be me?

Judgmental comments
Pierce my ears

Judgmental
Condescending eyes
Dirty looks

It seems my bae
found a new bae
that ain't me

Everyone moves on
without me.

No one sticks around
to ride the waves of life with me;
They just stop hitting me up,
They just leave.

What makes people stay?

Giving them their own way
A healthy hookup of
give and take,
heavily weighted compromise.

Look me in the eyes
See the betrayal
The frustration

The bitterness of being
through the ringer
Seeing things no young human
should; not saying things I wished
I would
Doing everything the critics
said I couldn't.

I know what they saying but I promise that
I'm cool tho
God says that I'm fearfully and wonderfully made
Plus he pays my bills, gives me chills, calms the thrills
pulsing through my veins

I'm enough for him
For now I'm content
Heaven will send

Me a man who
loves me the same

Worships Jesus
Loves me tenderly
Fanboys my writing
Kisses me softly in public

Hardly can stand the thought
of waking up without me
Entangled in sheets

Swaddled in love,
Just us becoming we.

Romances me
Sweeps me off my feet
Just with the way
He enunciates my name

Each syllable
a chord in
the love song;
the love story.

A girl can dream
even if she never sleeps.
You must have an
xylophone
in your belly
because
every sentence
you symphonize
Each phrase
rings in my ears
on the right key

Making it hard to forget
your melody
Like a radio earworm
on repeat

I'm stuck between killing myself
or them
Since either one of us is

better off dead.

I'm less interested
in the chase of having someone
More interested in someone
who relentlessly pursues me.

Oppressed by a system
that tracks my every move
just to prove
I'm worth the cost of EBT

College graduate;
worthless degree
Not in the talking stage
with anyone
as I mentioned before
bae got a new bae

So I showed him
the door
The most talking I do
with anyone;
the drive-thru
window
at Dunkin Donuts.

All fat; no luck
My own ghetto
Starbucks.

I'm loving this detox.
Have you ever drank

kale through a straw
so the scale number
wasn't so raw and ruthless?

Swimsuit season
Fast Approaching
Sweeping in faster
Than Florida humidity
in April

Wonder what a cold season is
As I thaw out from the ice just served to me
In the look my sister just steered straight for me
Like a Zamboni with no brakes

All caked on make-up
No true face.

Guess I've got to let go of you;
The idea of you and I.
Not yet a we.
Separated by pride;
Stubborn point of view.

My thoughts have made my head
Heavy
Lately you've been on my mind
though we haven't spoken in years

All your fault
must be another pride
thing
I should have never

written
you that letter
With that letter in your hand
I severed our good karma
positive vibes

I never got a hello or goodbye
you just stopped coming to my
neighborhood
Most likely because you don't want
the invisible leprosy
I have all over me
It's so contagious
It's affected my mind

My perception
of me

Am I really being myself or fooling myself
to think
this is the lie I want to live

Did I ever
Have a choice?

SOCIAL REJECTION

Muzzle me
with your ignorance
Read my message
but don't reply
Unfollow me
on every platform

I don't care.

Last I checked
the only way into heaven
is due to my faith in Jesus.

So what I choose to
keep my clothes on
instead of posting a topless
photo
on Instagram

Maybe that's what I am fighting for.

Maybe I am fighting to be heard.
Sick and Tired of Silence.
I have a voice.
I have beliefs.
And I'm tired of everyone just patting my head and saying,
"Aww you are so sweet."

My sweetness gone sour

Now is the hour
I refuse to be silent
ANYMORE.

Sorry I won't bend
and bow my knee
to your false
ideologies,
societal pressures,
and idolatry
of legalized sin.

I choose greatness
I choose to keep my top on,
my eyes on my cup at all times
my legs closed
my nose in a book

So I can learn higher thoughts
so I can aim for higher ways
to live each and every day

So I can be an example
of all that HE teaches me

It's pretty freaking low
of you
to make me nothing more
than the box next to a name
on a mother freaking
ballot.

Drops Mic.

ANGEL IN RED

A micropoem written after seeing a picture of myself in a red dress

This may look like a
young girl
in a pretty dress
but
she isn't a damsel
in distress.

She's a warrior
a rose
constantly
blooming
never assuming
the work for those
she clears the path for
will know her name
nor her strength
but she carries on.

Along a path
not yet tread
She's well-versed
and well-read

And yes,
she looks
damn good

in red.

OUT OF THE WOODS

Tired of not seeing the forest for the trees
when it comes to you
I would cut down every tree to get to you
but you would only call it wasted paper.

I tell everyone you are my world,
the sun, the moon
all while diminishing my own star
in order to keep you shining.

Why do I hold on
when you leave me
standing in the cold
with nothing to cover me
but a single feather.

Loving you is tough
lust and leather
that doesn't withstand
the weather;
my skin sweats
and sticks to you
uncomfortably.

Cubic zirconium
when I wanted
a diamond ring
on my left hand.

A green remnant
reminds me that
all that glitters isn't gold.

To have and to hold
Nothing holding me
but fear and unbelief

Not even
a prayer and sacrifice
can save me
Religious ritual;
no faith.

I hold your picture in my hands
so hard I bleed
but you have no interest in phlebotomy.

Or me.

It's you I idolize yet
all you ever do is cut me down to size
Loving you is no prize
And frankly my dear

I'm tired of all the wasted time.

FIGHT ON, FIGHTER

Chin up, soldier
I see you
I know you.

You once had
Stars in your eyes;
Saw love as a rose
Instead of a thorn.

You once burned the town down
Singlehandedly
With the fire in your eyes

Yet, life has gripped you
By the shirt collar,
Mocked you,
Thrown you away

And
   D
     O
       W
         N
A twisted rabbit hole
Of all your nightmares
Come true.

Don't you dare let the demons win;
Steal the joy
You can't seem to find
When you hold a purple pen
To paper.

You hold that pen to paper
Until the tears
Wash the rain clouds
From your eyes.

See the God damn diamond
You are
Your beauty is rare
And not always
Acknowledged.
If they talk over you
as they duct tape
your mouth shut.

Write your way
Out of the shadows
And let the light in.

How do I know this?
I know because I am you.

Believe in the glory.
Fire and fury.

The light is you.

BLANK CANVAS

Words on paper
what if the only way
of saying "I Was Here"
is putting words on lines
previously uninked.

Scattered tears
scattered thoughts
spilled ink
gently stirred with
blood, sweat, and irrational fears

Some people use labels to clarify
and communicate
identity of being a person.

Me?
I let the struggle speak for itself.

Chaotic madness
is my point of view
Beautiful disaster to the masses
and curious bystander.

So far no one else hears the voices
in my head quite as loudly
if they aren't placed on paper.

When I don't express what the voices say

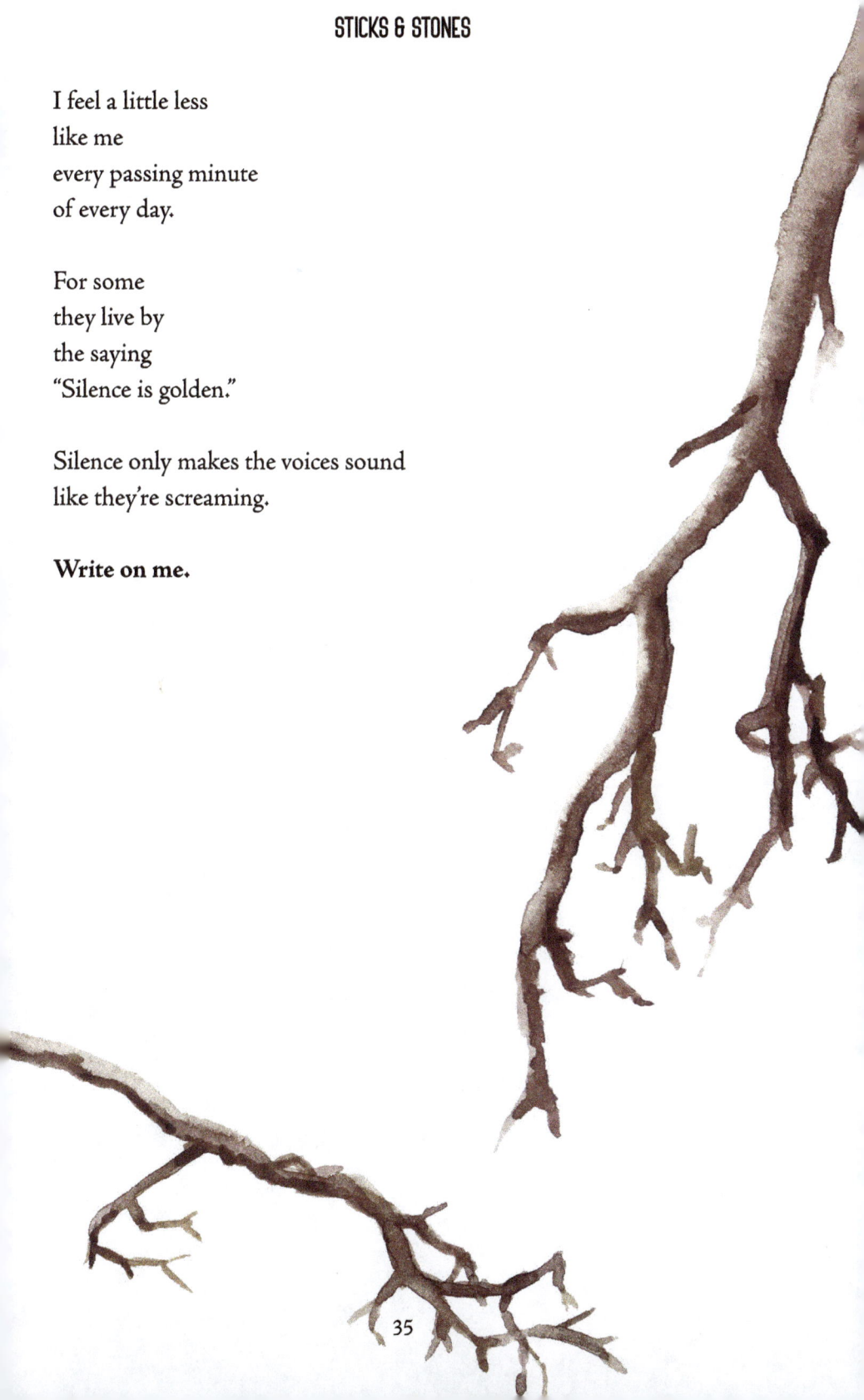

I feel a little less
like me
every passing minute
of every day.

For some
they live by
the saying
"Silence is golden."

Silence only makes the voices sound
like they're screaming.

Write on me.

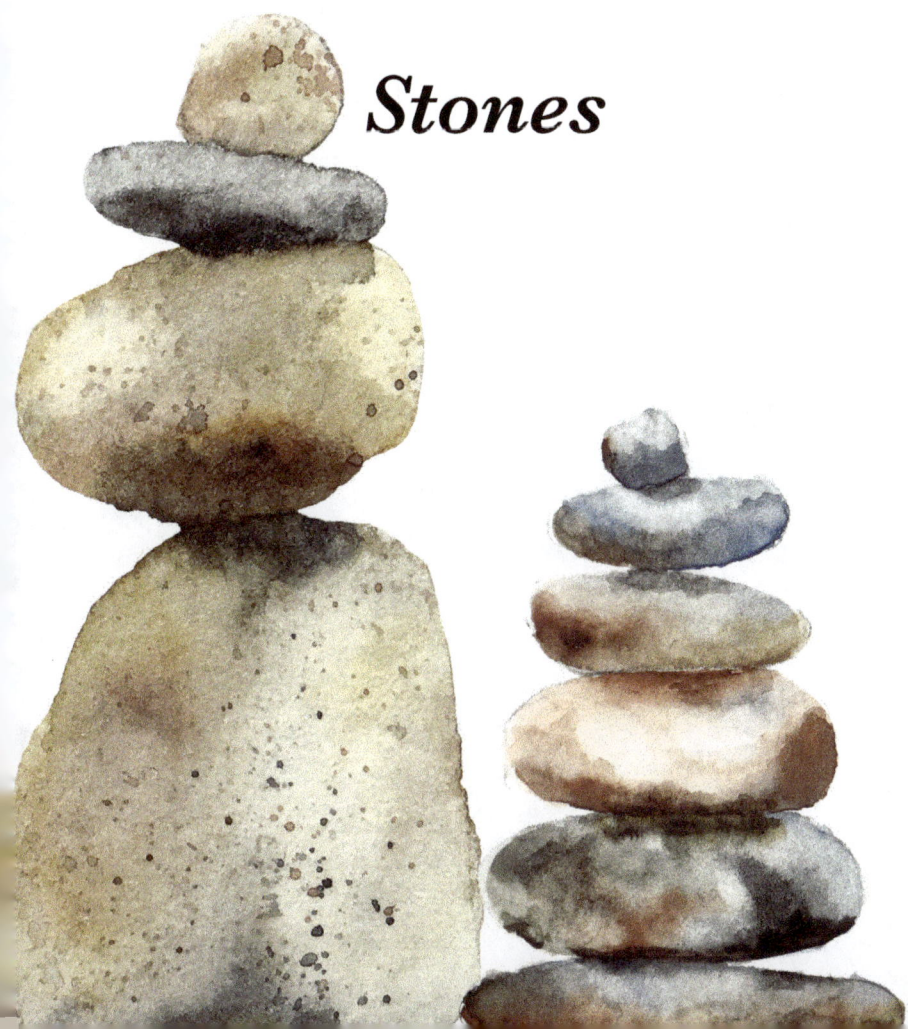

PART 2

Stones

To love someone means to see them as God intended them.—
Fyodor Dostoyevsky
Do things for people not because of who they are or what they do in return,
but because of who you are.
— Harold S. Kushner

Truth will ultimately prevail where there is pains taken to bring it to
light.— George Washington

The limits of tyrants are prescribed by the endurance of those whom they
oppress.— Frederick Douglas

Stones:

N.: hard solid nonmetallic mineral matter of which rock is made, especially as a building material.

V: throw stones at.

Example: I had to swallow the truth like a cold hard stone that even if he cared, he walked away.

Uses: in construction of houses and in the shaping and cutting of most diamonds sold in jewelry stores.

Example: You threw stones at me and I used it to reshape my life and shine like the diamond I am.

FISH OUT OF WATER

When I was younger
My favorite thing to do
In the swimming pool
Was see
How long I could

Hold my breath.

I wanted to be
Like the captivating
Yet mysterious
Mermaids
At Weeki Wachee Springs.

Free to float among the bottom
Of the revine
With the colorful fish
natural fauna.

Spring forward to adulthood
And I'm still swimming against
The current.

Some days it drags me under
But I've settled in
To the art of drifting
With the ebb and flow
Of the rising tide.

I've settled in
To the moments
I can't breathe
Because I know
Like the tide
I will rise

And
Glorify
The Creator
For making me this way

A fish out of water.

*mermaid

He was a man of the sea
So it
Makes sense
How he didn't run
When he spotted my sparkly scales
Along the length of my tail
Or
How I got bored in the shallow end

He was unafraid of
the mermaid in me.

DROWNING IN AN OCEAN OF NO TOMORROWS

They say that the love that happens to you out of nowhere, the lightening that you feel striking you twice, that's the love that you have to be careful of.

I didn't see him coming. As a matter of fact, the day I interviewed for the blowjob of jobs I couldn't even see him that well.

I was interviewing with S, and she was showing me the shop, yet the lights were out, so I didn't even notice that there was someone there.

If she hadn't pointed him out, I wouldn't have realized that he was there. Yet when I saw his face for that small instant, my heart leapt into my chest.

Ok, he's cute. So what? He's probably married I thought. In the dark, I couldn't even see that he was young. I thought he was over thirty.

She introduced him, "This is K our lead tech."

He smiled and said, "I'm the guy who's always here."

The first day that I showed up for the job, I don't remember his being there, but I do remember realizing what bullshit that job was going to be and wondering if I could make it work. I mean I had just gotten through a year of working as a hostess for little more than minimum wage while the servers I worked with had made fun of me and talked about me in the back of the restaurant. And I made that work. As a matter of fact, when I left, they had all said that they were going to miss me and that I was quickly going to see how much I would miss them. Instantly, I felt like I was a ghost. No one had said good morning or had made me feel welcome for those first few months. Despite my heart's begging me to quit, I didn't want to quit just yet.

The second day that I worked there foretold the events of the entire ten months in one small moment:

Customers came up to pay, and instead of being around to train me, S kept her fat ass in her desk chair because I guess the indent it left just sucked her in.

K walked into the office then, and I said, "Do you know what to do?"

He said nothing. He just helped me.

Instantly, I saw his heart, and I was impressed, and I was grateful someone had made me feel welcome.

Then he said, "Go get S, and she'll show you the rest."

Then, he smiled at me, and for one breath of a moment, it felt as if everything else had faded away, and I liked that my first impression of this young man had been right.

His heart was pure which meant that they were going to eat him alive, these wolves with whom we worked alongside.

Eat him alive they did. They were constantly body shaming him, making fun of how he wore Crocs to work, and that he frequented Wendy's for lunch.

"I told K he had to walk and couldn't ride on the golf cart because he may tip it over," The GM snickered one day after a short run to the front of the lot to fix the flag pole that ironically took four men and a golf cart.

A few days later, he had to tell me about the status of a customer's RV windows, and as he started to talk, he stuttered.

He quickly looked away and mumbled, "Christ." This was K's instant fix for whenever he felt foolish. Saying "Christ" was his reset button when he couldn't understand why he did something or honestly didn't know what else to say.

I thought it was cute. Then, when I was on the phone, and K was in my office, I started noticing that he was looking at me a lot. One day, he and the other techs were standing in the lobby of the office, and I answered the phone, and we made eye contact for a minute, and K didn't look away.

On Valentine's Day 2019, I bought the entire staff two dozen donuts and each member of the fourteen- person staff Valentines that contained $5 gift cards so that they could get coffee or something to eat.

Each Valentine was addressed to each guy and was signed by me. I chose what each guy's card would say. Yet I decided K's would express a hint of my feelings.

His said, "You complete me;" and it was 100% true. I wouldn't have survived that place without him and his friendship.

As I began working alongside him, I saw a broken and unhappy young man. It turned out that he was about a year and a half younger than I was, and one of the other window techs told me that he'd been with the same girl for three years, but if he was in such a loving, happy relationship, why wasn't he more passionate about life?

So before then, I began praying for every person on the staff by name in the morning before I left for work, but at night I prayed a specific prayer for K. One that would help him to see his potential, to feel more confident in who God had made him— to see that God had healed him from all the pains of the past.

As he was leaving that Thursday afternoon, when I handed him the Valentine, his whole face lit up, and he even blushed.

I was still feeling ghostly, and as on every day, I was dying inside sitting at this desk listening to the way the manager and his family talked about everyone.

Music helped until my computer stopped working properly. I asked them about getting a new one, and they shrugged it off and said that I just needed to defrag the hard drive.

I started bringing the laptop I had gotten from living on campus at Saint Leo University, and then comments about that started. The abuse I had to endure at the hands of this family was mind blowing.

In January of 2019, R mentioned that my relationship status had everybody up in arms: "Everyone is going crazy trying to figure out if you are single or not."

I had never worked anywhere where a significant other was of concern as to whether or not I was capable of doing my very simple job.

February 21, 2019: It was Thursday. There was an incident with a customer who was dissatisfied with something on this coach. I should have kept my mouth shut and let the chips fall where they might, but this was when I still cared about this job, so I grabbed K and told him what was going on, and he said to tell R that he should head over there and check it out. Technically, K should have gone there himself and inspected the coach. I texted R but got no answer. Those customers came back into the office, and I ran down the hallway to find S. I did all I could. It was time for management to take over and to do their jobs. I popped into T's doorway and was surprised to see that he had been in his office the entire time and could easily have stepped in and resolved the matter.

"Do you know where your mom is?" I asked him.

"I have no idea," T said.

I went back into the shop and grabbed K for the second time. By now, he was as irritated as I was that no one was doing anything about this.

He spoke to the customer and reassured the husband and wife that we were sending someone out to the coach.

Yet the wife asked to speak with a manager, so K told me to call R in order to track him down, and at the same time called down the hallway for S, who had been in the GM's office the entire time and could have taken care of it anytime, but the prince and the queen of this horrible establishment didn't think they owed anyone anything including helping their customers to resolve an obvious issue.

R said to me one day at the end of my shift, "You would be dangerous if you stopped drinking beer" which indicated that he disapproved of my taste in adult beverages and also the fact that I was constantly mocked by men for my little "beer gut." Some male customers even kept asking me if I was expecting. It's more of a posture issue and less of an insult but really why must men ask that? Are they trying to say I would look "cute" with child?

I swallowed my pride and let it slide, but it showed me that this place was laden with toxic masculinity and body shaming.

Sometime near the end of February, R asked me to help him in the supply closet which was locked and which only office staff had keys for. I helped him, and the phone rang, and since there was a phone in there, I answered it. While I was on the phone, he grabbed me from behind, and I felt sexually harassed. I couldn't let anyone know because they wouldn't have believed me. There was no HR representative for this company.

S had taken the phone out of my hands several times while I had been on a call with a customer. The first time I thought nothing of it because of her extreme OCPD issues, but when it happened multiple times, I regretted not confronting her about it because it was completely out of line. It seemed that the reason behind this aggressive supervisor behavior was so that S could step in and re-do things for the sake of her getting the credit which begs the question: what do you need me for?

Another time in the early months when I was just learning about how to properly document a drop-off RV window unit, a delivery driver was in the office with the paperwork that he had to give me so that I could fill out more paperwork so that everything was documented about his units. When I was writing something on the paper in front of him, he made a comment that my handwriting was some of the nicest he had seen anywhere.

Before I could even thank him for the compliment, S took credit for my handwriting and claimed that she had trained me in that too. I looked at her like *what the actual fuck?* And it was on this Friday in February when I became very much aware that I wasn't the only one in this office with mental illness since I've been plagued with anxiety and depression since I was about twelve years young. I'm no doctor but I can recognize someone's silently crying for help when I see them.

I drafted my resignation letter on April 22, but I vowed that I would only stay to watch over these guys that work on the windows. The GM even threw his dog's feces in K's trash can multiple times, and he laughed about it.

Once in late May or early June the GM specifically said to me, "Don't tell K I gave you this." He handed me $60 cash. Before leaving, I put $30 in the tip jar for the crew of window techs and glass experts. Before clocking out, S found the tip and realized that I had put it in there, and she handed it back to me saying that the GM had given it to me to spend on myself and that I shouldn't give it to the guys so that they could waste it on cheeseburgers.

In the start of the slow season, the whiteboard in the warehouse was not clearing. The ink was sticking to the surface due to the fact that we live in Florida, and whiteboards are meant to be in a cool, dry area. The heat was causing the purple marker I had been using to remain visible.

One Friday, two hours before I was set to clock out for the day, S ripped the whiteboard down from the hook it was stored on in the warehouse, and she cleaned it in the conference room so she could sit down while she did it.

And as she always did if she had to do anything other than gossip, help someone or incessantly check Snapchat, she threw a freaking fit.

"This purple marker is not coming off. Now I have to redraw all the lines on here and start over. No more purple marker!" She began yelling in the office.

All the guys were in there and heard her. Everyone on staff knew who used purple marker. She was once again blaming me for having to clean something. I'm surprised she didn't blame me for global warming or for homelessness.

None of the guys defended me but instead, they all clocked out. They were not Norman Bates and had had enough of this psycho.

Me? I had to stay there and endure this as she not only made a huge scene because I had used purple marker but also told me that no one could use it.

On the following Monday, when K went to write something on the board, he popped his head into my office from the shop and asked,

"What colors are we allowed to use?"

"Oh, you know, black and blue. It's supposed to resemble a bruise."

K smirked at me as he got the joke and walked out.

About two weeks later, S said we could try using purple marker on the board, and I looked up solutions for cleaning stubborn dry erase marker off the board. It turned out that toothpaste not only cleans stains off your teeth, but it also helps clean off just about anything including coffee stains on your mugs and dry erase marker that won't erase.

I also relayed that information to K because I thought he would remember its being funny.

I didn't want to fall in love with a guy who went home to someone else, but it just swept me under like an invisible current. They tell you about the dangers of riptide, but no one warns you that you could be swept down into the riptide of who someone else is.

As we started to joke around more and to get comfortable with each other as coworkers, I never expected how quickly I would fall into his way of being:

+How his laugh sounded like a sweet symphony

+How he muttered "Christ" when he didn't know what else to say

+I even remember a Friday afternoon when he thought no one could hear him while he was working in the shop. He started singing Happier by Bastille.

I set out to show him that a love that's true is selfless; it builds up; it encourages; it inspires.

I watched this beautiful but brooding young man go from miserable to laughing louder, to being more confident in his abilities, and even

49

to taking pride in his appearance. I watched him begin to dress up a little. He went from having a goatee to shaving and to cutting his long mop of brown curls.

Yet, the only indications that I had had that he had felt something for me were subtle but hard to ignore:
  ♦He called me pretty in front of a customer.
  ♦He pranked me with the shop door.
  ♦He listened to the music I suggested when he could have just ignored it.
  ♦He smiled at me often with all of his teeth.
  ♦He once said, "I saved the day" because I had fixed the time clock.

After I gave him the Valentine, he saw me talking to a customer whose tone dripped with personal interest in me.

K walked back in when the guy walked out and said, "Who was that guy?"

I explained that he was a customer, and he said, "Oh. He's outside pacing back and forth."

Maybe I read something into it, maybe I created a love story in my head destined for a Jack Dawson and Rose from Titanic ending, but the heart wants what it wants.

One thing I can say about caring about K is that he was the first guy who ever asked me to repeat what I had said, even if it was in a whisper.

There was a day when S was yelling like a loon about something, and I shook my head in disgust.

I heard K yell out, "No," and I was blown away that he had seen my non-verbal cue.

I guess I fell in love with him in order to cope with the abuse, to keep my head above water, to feel anything at all since it had been four years since I had felt love for any guy at all.

As the smell of dead rats drifted around us, we both swam toward shore as the waves of this toxic workplace and the political abusive mind games crashed all around us, and the wreckage of our sinking boat cascaded farther and farther away.

We both clung to this unspoken subterfuge between us which I felt gave us a sense of sanity and at the same time, frightened us because it was something neither of us was expecting to happen at all.

For ten months, I showed up at a job I couldn't stand because I realized nothing meant more to me than taking care of that young man and making sure that he and the entire staff felt valued and appreciated for their hard work in the face of such coyote uglies.

I learned a lot about myself, about love, and about the value, dignity, and enduring strength of the human spirit, all because I decided to stay and cherish the beauty in the ashes of this short-lived but very powerful friendship between K and me.

We ended abruptly. He started by rolling his eyes whenever I talked to him or by not saying goodbye when he left.

He told me he was getting his own place, but I found out later that he was getting his own place with his girlfriend and her best friend with two kids, a two-bedroom apartment.

The day I realized my time at the job had ended, he told me that his girlfriend was bringing her bedroom set.

The same day, I got a note saying that I was being put on a 30-day probation for being myself. Writing, reading, and doing work for my own business.

Two weeks after I left, I texted him:

Thank you for everything, Mr. Suncoast.

He didn't reply.

My heart ached for the synchronicity that we had had without thought, for what we had lost.

+Our taste in music

+Our love for the outdoors and specifically for the ocean.

+How we each had the same sense of humor.

+His love of BMX and my love of skateboarding

Recently out of the blue, his face popped up on my phone as "someone you may know" on Facebook. And it happened when I first turned my phone on; I wasn't on the Facebook app at all.

My sister was our mutual friend.

I added him just to see if what we had had was real, if I had meant anything to him or not.

That night I checked Facebook and found that he had blocked me.

I don't regret what I felt for him or anything that I had shared with him.

He had made his choice. And I wasn't it.

I wish that I could have saved him from the chains that bound him or from settling down with someone he didn't really love or from feeling moody and miserable.

Yet, I respect him for the choice he made. I admire him for all he is, but I had fallen in love with an enigma.

One question still haunts me at night: If I had never loved him, would I have made it back to shore alive?

For more on Mr. Suncoast:

Who Is Mr Suncoast
5K views · 1 year ago

Chelsea DeVries

This is an hour and fourteen minutes long but it's the other half of the story. This is the story about Mr. Suncoast recently shouted ...

Long before I had the money to visit a counselor, I had all these unacknowledged secrets and feelings and May 6, 2020 I decided to share them in a backstory video on my Youtube channel.

Hear me share the entire unfiltered story in this hour-long video.

And thank you for 5,000 views.

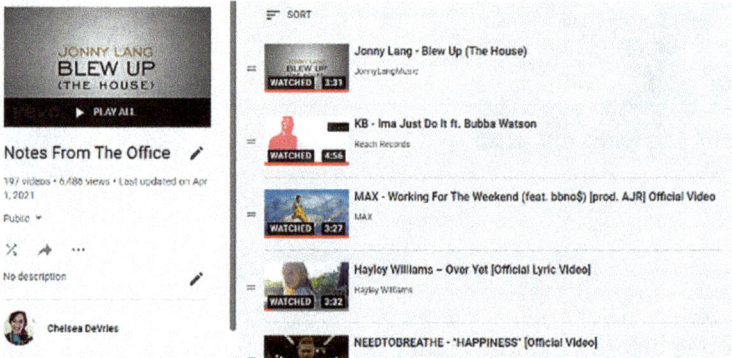

And for the playlist I kept jamming to help me stay alive
While working there

After being at that job for two months I decorated my office with quotes that I felt would serve as notes to self, and one of them I had up the entire duration of time I worked there.

"You will be too much for some people, those aren't your people."

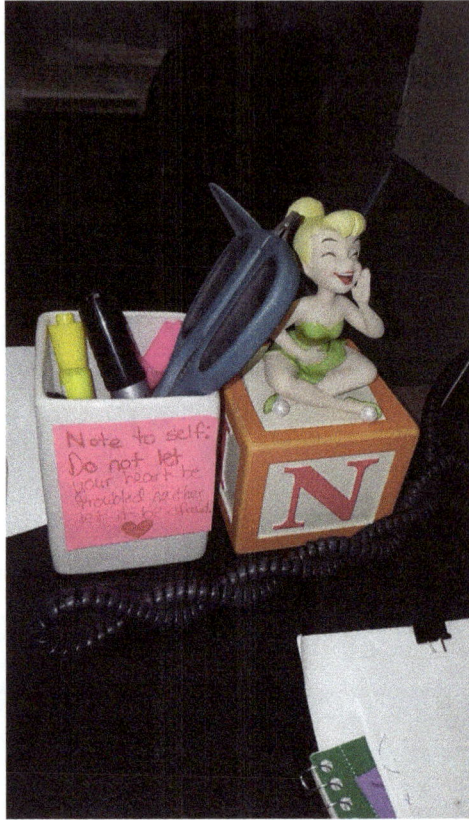

After I was sexually harassed by one of my co-workers, I placed my keys in this collectible Tinkerbell storage box in order to avoid walking each of the other window techs to the supply closet to avoid any other incidences and to increase productivity within the workplace. Only a few weeks later, my boss and his wife made a rule that all window techs had to be walked to the supply closet and be let in by anyone who had a key which meant I no longer could keep my keys within here in order to avoid any possible chance of another sexual harassment taking place. Ironically enough, this box almost fell completely off my desk near the end of a work day and in a moment of pure heroic adrenaline, Mr. Suncoast happened to be standing there and he stuck out his Croc and caught it otherwise Tinkerbell would have met a much less pleasant fate.

Most of my glory moments at this oppressive job were that a customer or several customers would always make it a point to show me appreciation for my hard work. This was hand-painted for me by a customer by the name of Bettey Hatch, an eighty-year-old redhead lady who came in for a quick window repair and who was everything I hope to become when I have the privilege of being that age. Being that I've never had a grandparent I was close to, she was like the grandmother I never had but had always wanted. Just a free-spirited courageous female with an artistic flair and a heart of gold.

Three days after I was set to quit for good, I held on and God had a lot of moments where he would show me things subliminally.

A customer came in and presented everyone at work that day with an ice cream. The brand: Bully's.

Obviously, God was trying to say to me:
You need to hold strong in the face of these bullies.

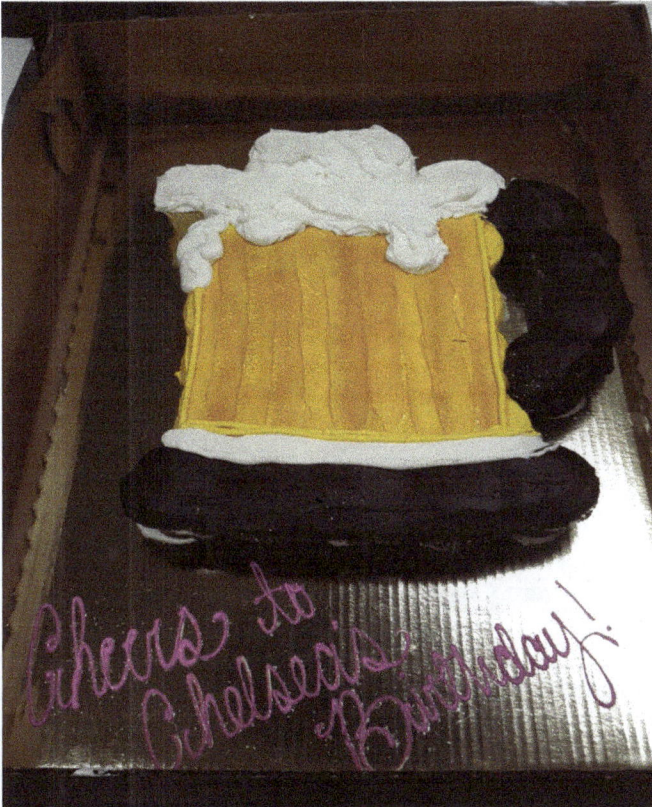

One of the last things I did for the guys prior to resigning because I had jokingly always promised to bring them beer to work was get this custom cupcake cake from Publix that resembled that beer I never got to have with them. I used the Friday before my birthday to present it to them. Honestly, I was the most stoked that I got to celebrate my birthday with all of them.

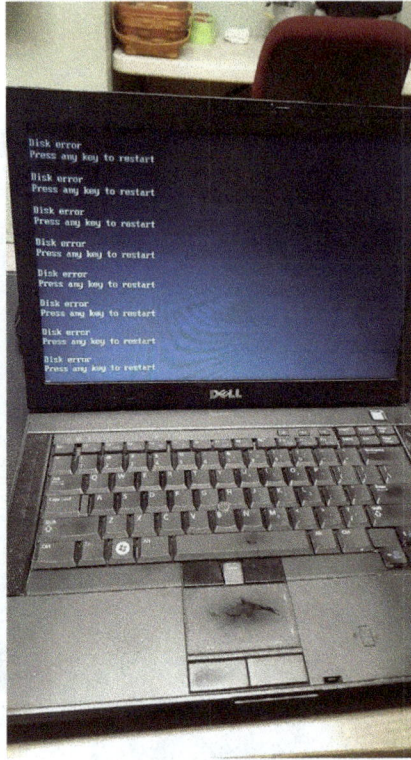

As my office computer stopped working properly and was slower than slow but I was the person customers went to with billing inquiries and who was entirely in charge of scheduling them for their repair appointments, I decided to bring my personal laptop to work with me. It was fine up until I brought it to the office. Then, it started acting up and eventually stopped keeping a secure LAN(which is tech savvy for a secure connection to WIFI even if WIFI was readily available) so my free refurbished sixth Saint Leo laptop died an untimely death because of someone sabotaging it's overall usage.

It was the first place I worked where your personal belongings were not safe. I mean, maybe it was the rats running across my desk when I wasn't there but I look back now and I see the glaring signs telling me: *You don't belong here.*

wittywriterpoet26

View Insights   Promote

Liked by **tscphilespr** and **6 others**

wittywriterpoet26 Feeling pretty under the office lights💜🍬🎉
#polishedbylaw #selfie... more

September 9, 2019

Towards the end of my last month there, I took this office selfie at the end of a workday following clocking out. As you can see, I was truly starting to feel confident in my own skin but at the same time, I was crawling out of it because the longer I was around the gossip, body shaming, family strife, toxicity in any and all forms, the more I felt the mask falling off my face, and the smile you see in the above photo wearing tired and thin.

Like A reflection
in a broken mirror

There is more to wrong with me
than right

I'm not sure anyone
will ever
understand me.

I keep reminding
myself
that
I am beautiful
worthy of love
enough
but despite the
madness
the chaos
underneath
these dimples.

My poem I called Broken Mirror written during a very toxic oppressive shift.

On September 25, 2019, I was harassed the entire eight-hour shift because of a story being passed around about me giving wrong information to a customer.

- S arrived to work very late and actually screamed at me because I had been in the bathroom instead of at my desk when she arrived.
- She asked me openly after calming down an hour after she arrived if the guys were treating me differently today.
- Right before asking me to clock out, S told me that I wasn't going to be paid for any overtime but her condescending tone felt to me like a direct threat that they may not pay me at all.

It was this shift that left me aware that my time at this job was very much over but it also made me completely eyes wide open that if I didn't get help as soon as possible...I may not live to see another day.

SOMEDAY MY PRINCE WILL COME; OVERRATED

"Lower your expectations"
I whisper to my heart as I clock in.

Yet, I still expect you
To speak up
To smile
To look at me with longing.

Like you've never been loved before
And you've fallen for the first time
Your heart has no broken edges or scars
Straight out of the factory
Right off the press

But instead you talk to me
Like I'm salt in your wounds
Vinegar on your lips in the hot summer heat
Lemon juice straight from the peel
Sour and nothing you desire

You crush my expectations
Of all we could ever be
With all that we aren't.

Mark my words.
You will fall for me
And you will fall hard.

I've already fallen for you
But still I will rise
Because guys see everything first and foremost
With their eyes
Then their heart.
Girls are smarter
we know looks fade
height diminishes with age
But still some of us
Wear our hearts on our sleeves
Like they are our crowns
And wonder ignorantly why
We lose track of how to smile
How to hold our head up
Or even to fall again

Because boys diminish a girl's light and shatter her crown
While men help her to rise victoriously and shine.

Wait for a king.
Someday my prince will come.
Overrated.

HEAVY HEART

Today I am sad
Like a wingless dove
As hard as she tries
She can't get above.

Above the idea
That she may
Never be loved
in the way she loves.

With her heart
Presented
In a pretty
Gold bow

Only to be placed
On a shelf marked,
"Just For Show."

I want that post love glow
Where without a shadow of a doubt
He just knows

"you're the one."

The way his eyes
Plug into yours
Says it all.

I've fallen and I can't get up
I fell for you
That handsome smile
That laugh that mimics music
The fact that you find my jokes
Funny at all.
Yet, you are too busy looking at she.

She will
Never be
Me.

You say you love her
But a part of me
Thinks,
Hopes,
Prays
It is only something you say
So she doesn't realize you are
Pulling away.

That is only
My naïve heart
Hoping someone
Would choose me for once.

Until then
I am not enough

I lay here on the floor
Like a wingless dove.

My chest is heavy

CHELSEA DEVRIES

From this bird that sits upon it
The weight of this burden
Too hefty to bare alone.

Will love ever love me?
This I am not certain.

HE CAN'T LOVE ME

They say the truth will set you free
Yet I never wanted to be free of you.

Your laugh sounded like music;
You read my unspoken cues.

We never admitted there was a spark between us
Unspoken but palpable
Unexpected subterfuge.

Loving you just happened
I still can't understand
It's rhyme or it's reason.

We once chatted
About music,
Now I'm left to feel blue.

Truth is
She may be all that you want
But I'm all that you need.

Thank you for what we shared
You were good to me.

I get it.
I do.
My mom called it too.

CHELSEA DEVRIES

She said you knew you weren't good enough
For me.

I can't understand why you would choose to hit
"Block Friend."

2020 has arrived
It's the truth I clearly see.

You set me free.
And it's time I choose me.

UNACKNOWLEDGED

I shouldn't be writing this
A psychic told me that
"Nothing would come from this situation."

A counselor told me not to feed you
With my thoughts or mental energy

I keep thinking about when I put a novel out
Should I acknowledge you and your seasonal
Part in my story?

It's this persistent picture that
keeps playing in my head.
I see your nickname on the page
Where you dedicate a book to someone.

How do you dedicate a book to someone who
blocked you on Facebook?
Ignores your texts?
Never offered an explanation
About why he no longer wanted to be friends with you?

Were you scared that I would beg you to love me?
I am sorry that I left without telling you
Why
That I would never blame you for the
Bad and evil things I witnessed and experienced
at the hands of someone
with envy in their heart

and greed stuck
between their tongue
and their teeth.

I didn't know what to say to you
I didn't know if you would
Tell me to stay or
be angry with me
Because
I saw them
For who they are
Instead of just pretending
I was dumb, deaf, and blind.

Gone is your musical laugh and the sparkle in your eyes
As you would smirk at me
With this synchronicity
You thought it was
All a ringless circus too.

The guy in the top hat
The Greatest Showman
No Hugh Jackman
He couldn't juggle,
Tell jokes,
Or tame a caged lion.

Spitting fire was his one and only talent
As the master of Ceremonies,
The elephant he rode
Would spray water from her trunk
Killing dreams, Hopes, and new ideas
Left and right

Unlike Dumbo,
She was angry because her ringmaster clipped
Her wings and convinced her she couldn't fly.

Fly she could but he kept her chained.
Chained and dependent on him
for bread, water, and a place to rest her head.

Yet, he would demean her
Keep her feeling small
So she always had to
Validate herself
In his eyes only…

It was a dark and dreary
Tim Burton movie
We were a part of
But like Zac Efron and Zendaya
In the Greatest Showman,
The characters we played
Were not convinced
Their love was enough
To make it.

Were you mad that I cared about you
Or were you mad because
there was nothing we could do about it?

Were you mad that I had the courage
And open door to grasp my freedom
Before they hung me
Like the witch they believed me to be?

I did care about you.
I was so thankful for you.
I think you are a beautiful person.
So ordinary but extraordinary all in one person.

So complex
Such an enigma.
To me, you will always be a mystery.

Our timing was neither wrong nor right.
You were good to me.
I encouraged you.
You made me feel heard.
You didn't look at me
For my body or physique.

Yet, whenever I looked at you
I felt ok to be me.
And for that,
I can't regret
How I fell for you
With no real
Motive or reason.
I just loved you.
I still love you.

But you won't talk to me.
So I guess I will write you the dedication
After all.

Because it feels better to acknowledge you
Then pretend you didn't matter to me.
That you still matter to me.

*That I don't think of you when I listen to Billie Eillish
And remember how I made you laugh because I said she may be a
        Satanist.*

She's not.
Yet, just the notion of that didn't make you
Flinch or judge me, and you never forget
Someone like that.

Someone who runs towards you and your outlandishness
Instead of away from it.
Someone who makes you repeat what you said
Even if you mumbled it because it deserved to be
Heard.

Someone who always helped me, talked to me,
And believed in me until you didn't.

Someone who I miss
Someone who I pray for every single day

Someone like YOU

You have to acknowledge someone like that.

Even if it was only a series of moments
they made an ordinary boring job
memorable.
Just the thought of you makes me look back
At those months of my life and smile.

Even with tears in my eyes.

I've let you go
but I just had to let you know
that I acknowledge
all you were to me and
all I hope you become.

Mr. Suncoast,
This is for you.

*a portion of this poem first appeared in a virtual quarantine gallery during
the 2020 COVID-19 pandemic. Check out theqgallery.com*

SELFLESS LOVE

Toxic
Love
Is
All
I've
Known.

I've been shown
Kindness
Until
I
Realized
They
Fed
Off This Notion
That I couldn't
Not acknowledge them.

People have used me for authenticity
My genuine heart and soul
My relentless mercy
My compassion

Yet instead of being angry
It makes me glad

All this time
They believed

They had the upper hand
But it was I who ran away from them.

Not the other way around.
I don't want companionship
Relationship
Or sexual vices.

I only want someone to tell me
Who I am is ok
And that you were grateful

That at the end of the day
I saw good in you

Even when no one else did.
Even when
You couldn't see it
In yourself.

GHOSTS OF MY PAST

Picture this
That orb ball in the Haunted mansion movie
It came to mind today
And
It got me thinking about you and me.

I still hope one day we can sit down like adults
And get the closure we deserve.

I see us meeting at a coffee shop
and expressing ourselves
with no judgmental eyes on us

Maybe we could find solace
With what happened
Maybe we will
Let what we buried
Rest in its grave.

But
Something should be said
About the fact that I thought about you
And a mansion full of ghosts today.

You are still haunting me
Which only means one of us
Has unfinished business
That we must air out

CHELSEA DEVRIES

The truth must be known so

Our chances of ever being together
Can rest in peace
Eternally.

ENIGMATIC ENERGY

I tried to manifest a text from you but
Our wires were malfunctioned;
Truth bomb defused.

You don't care about me
In the same way
I care about you.

Yet, I still love you
And I hope you thought of texting me
Even if you didn't.

Because we left a lot unsaid
Even though you left me on read

I can't unsend my love to you.

It was delivered and received
Even if it wasn't reciprocated.

I sit here
Still bleeding internally
for you

To manifest
Back into my life.

OUR TIMING

Our timing
Is all wrong
Like church bells
That toll too long.

They ring in my ears and I fail
To hear another sound.

Our timing is all right
Weirdly enough

In saving you
Or attempting to

I've saved myself.
My life has meaning
Purpose
Passion
A reason to keep breathing
Believing
In You.

No question
But
There may never be an "us."

That causes tears to fall
From my eyes

Quickly becoming
Salt dust.

Our timing
Is neither
Wrong nor right

You saved me
I saved you
And we both
Remain
Alive.

FOOL FOR YOU

Someone today
told me not to dedicate a book to you
and I balled my eyes out.

I truly believe I would rather love you
even if I end up alone
than feel nothing at all

Why do people think they can tell me how to live,
who to love,
how to feel?

I mean
for ten months
I was basically
dead inside
and not one person.
Not even my family
smelt the stink
of my rotting
flesh
the stench
of my grave clothes
the formaldyhyde
perfume
I wore.

I love you

I love you
I love you

Why can't that be enough?

Why must I prove myself to everyone and anyone with everything?
I'm happy loving you
Why can't they let me be happy?

Why must they try to shine a light on
the sad truth
that you don't care
and you never did

And I'm an absolute fool
for still caring
still hanging on

like who I am isn't worthy of your love?

I just want to love you
That's all I want to do.
That's all I'm going to do.

Until you realize you love me.

SEEKING CLARITY

Last night I came to a conclusion
You and I were an illusion
We made sense
Physically
Spiritually
Mentally
Emotionally

You may be my twin flame

But keeping this fire ablaze is burning me down
In the worst way
And
I don't want to ruin
All the good
You gave me

You made me feel valued
Heard
Believed

But you didn't believe in us.

So I guess I must
Realize that
I must be okay without you.

I am going to do this life thing alone

STICKS & STONES

Plain and simple
Because no one will ever hold a flame to you

Famous or not
I will never love again.

RAZOR BLADES

Trigger warning: This poem contains imagery that directly correlates to suicide.

From November 26, 2018 to September 30, 2019 I worked at a place that illusively looked like my dream job. It was full-time, close to home, and I would work in an office.

Once we rang in the New Year, I was rung out like a wet rag and the truth dripped out of me.

The abuse started.
Then, the sexual harassment.
Then I had to witness my coworkers also be harassed, body shamed, and demeaned.

Yet, while working there I met a young man who was kind to me from the second day until the day I resigned, and it was our effortless friend-ship that kept me alive.

I never told anyone; him or anyone there, or even shared this with any-one publicly but we had a supply closet in the middle of the office full to the brim with tools to work on RV windows.

One of which were pure, straight edge industrial strength razor blades.

And I actually envisioned myself several times just walking inside the closet and using the blades to end my life.

Reading All The Bright Places by Jennifer Niven recently brought this poem out of me and helped me find strength to share my story. I resigned and sought help and now am being treated for my anxiety and depression.

That guy no longer speaks to me but I will always believe if he didn't befriend me, I may not still be alive to this day.

So I wrote this poem in order to share my truth (blunt and very vivid as it may be) and also tell anyone out there struggling, find anyone you absolutely trust and reach out.

Your story isn't over yet.

RAZOR BLADES

You cut me out of your life
But right now
I wish you could text me

Or
That I could send a pic
And we could reminisce
About the times when we were good.

I am telling you this now
Although I've never told anyone else
But when we worked together

The pull of my love for you
Made me feel
Sparks
Flames
Fireworks

Inside me

Match or not
You lit me up

I found me
The real me
In your eyes.

Yet, the weight of
The hate
The envy
The lies
This idea
That I am not enough

Made me
Think
That
Maybe this world
Would be better
Off without me.

This isn't the first time
this has happened to me.
At 12
At 21
And 28.
The people around me
no longer want me
and if they do,
they sure have a shitty way
of showing it.

Supressed secrets
And truths
Cut you from the
Inside out

Razor blades
In the
Supply closet

Over each of my wrists
Sliver each vein
With a twist

Bleeding out
I wondered
If you would
Whisper
One last time

How much you loved me.

Inspired by All The Bright Places by Jennifer Niven
"I am broken. I am a fraud. I am impossible to love."

YOU WOULD NEVER BELIEVE THIS

Since I last saw you
I called into a radio station
And
Got on the air
All in the name
Of
Hot Chelle Rae

I've read 1,000 pages
I'm getting better at making Youtube videos
People actually watch

Maybe not talking to you
Or
Seeing you
Is giving me more to say

And this uninhibited nerve
To be myself boldly.

Today, my sister told me to forget you.

Funny
I couldn't if I tried.

You left a mark on me
And I won't waste
One single breath

Pretending
You don't exist.

Or that you aren't
The reason I feel free to be me.

You were the booster to my rocket;
It would be foolish to try to knock it.

Maybe one of these days
The me that I am
Will meet a man
Who chooses me

Unlike you
Who cut ties
When the going was good.

Forget him
She said.

Believe me, sis.
I wish I could.

HEART VERSUS MIND

Today I miss your face
Despite the fact that
you made me chase you.

Only to turn around
And settle in with her.

I still don't understand
Why
My heart chose you
And chooses you still
Even after you and I haven't spoken in months.

The last thing you texted me
Was
"Who is this?"

And the more I focus on
What makes someone
Who seemed to "get me"
Better than even my own family
Turn around and act like
We are strangers

The stranger I find love.

Why do we spend so much
effort
    time
       and thought
On those who don't do the same for us?
Still I wish I could text you right now
Or I could see you in person

I would salute you
Like you always did
When you clocked out

Like I was a valiant soldier
And you were in awe of me

Like a hometown war hero,
We were stationed for different battlefields

The worst part is my heart is convinced
That you are the key to silencing
This battlefield in my mind.

I wish my heart would forget you
But instead she hopes she will find you again

Until then,
To honor you,
To every battlefield,
Your face I must carry
And I promise to always
Soldier on.

Inspired by "The 1" by Taylor Swift

PAPERCUTS AND BROKEN HEARTS

I read men like books
Every page has
Something
New to
Teach me.

Yet, all men ever do is lust me.
They never love me.

I don't want a man who lusts me
I want to be loved for me.

Love and trusted
Not used
Abused
For an ego boost
Then ghosted.

You can't tell me there is no difference.

Sex doesn't equal love
Babies don't mean stability.

I read you much too fast
And turned your pages
Like a trashy romance
Insatiably
And

Ignorantly.

When you left

It made
Sense
That
My
Fingers
were all bloody.

ASEXUAL POEM

Take it off
Give me some head
Thrown on the bed

Low cut blouse
Cut the cake

Handcuffs
Nipple tassels

Sounds remorseful
Regretful
Unfortunately for me
Not you
Quite the hassle.

No emotions
Just motions
Of up, down, and again.

You want me,
You need me,

Fuck me,
My friend.

Vomit
Comet

It's done
It's over.
The end.

Written for anyone who identifies as asexual, demisexual, or a combination of both

STOP SCROLLING; START LIVING

Comparison
Is a tool
Of the enemy.

Social media
Is nothing
But a façade.

It turns out
We all stalk our ex lovers
Until we're blue in the face.

Facebook is fake.

I don't consider you my friend.

Envy is empty.

Get out
And
LIVE.

WHAT I MEANT BY THANKS FOR THE OPPORTUNITY

I meant
No harm
By resigning.

I had no choice.

I had to resign
From this illusive
Idea you had of me

In your mind
I was a china doll
Who
Wasn't allowed to crack

Under the pressure
From the heat
Of the office lights

Or the hot and sharp
Sound
Of the boss's wife
Breathing
      Down
          My Neck.

I would have let you
Decapitate me
In your guillotine

If it meant
I had a few
More moments

Soaking in
The sunshine

Of that boy
In the Crocs'
Laugh
Smile
Sense of humor
Way of being.

Just an Elton John
Ready and willing
To crocodile rock

And I will
Forever
Be his
Number one fan.

NEVER ENOUGH; MISTAKE

I stand corrected
Every time.

They patronize me
They tell me my mistakes
Are a reflection
Of who I am.

As if I must lay in the muck
They try to fuck me
with.

This idea
That everything must be done
By the books

The numbers are backwards
Logical dyslexia
Naivete
Stop being such a puppy at play.

"Stop being so happy."

It irritates me

Is all I can hear
When someone tries to tell me

This
Is
The
Only
Way
It
Should be done

Progression is a sin unless it's used
to further a political or radical agenda.

MS. LONELY

I've never held hands
Kissed lips
Or
Celebrated a special day

With anyone.

People say
I'm too picky
I'm too prude
I'm too broken.

There have been close calls
And siren songs
Almost lovers
Never more than one sided
Covers

Almost lovers
Who
Flirted
Fingered
And
Fell out of love
With my pride

They left me
When I needed them most

It was most convenient for them.

So many men
In my DMs.

Shooting shots
And
Getting shot down

All in less than a moment

Why?

Because they place me
In a pretty box
Make it all about my looks

When I would rather fall in love
With a man
Who knows Jesus
And
loves reading books.

THOUGHTS WHILE HAVING A PANIC ATTACK

Have yet to make it to the counselor
But
I can barely breathe

I can't seem to swallow
The painful truth

That you up and left me
Betrayed me

Settled for lust
Instead of love

I still don't
Understand
Why the fuck

You left me
Didn't choose me
Were more foe
Than friend

In the end

I wanted to be
Right about you.

After all,

They can't be
Right
When they say
SCREAM
S
  H
    O
      U
        T
At me

LOVE IS BLIND.
He was the wrong one.
Or
He was right
Yet
You met at the wrong time.

WHAT IF

Bear with me
As I
Come off crazy to most
But
What if you still miss me?
What if you did feel for me?
What if you only blocked me
To protect me
And you

You wouldn't lose your job.
They couldn't hold this over you.

What if you still think highly of me
Despite the trauma bond
PTSD
Mental breakdown
Or
Suicide ideation?

What if you still hear my voice in your head
When you feel like a failure
Or wish you were dead?

Maybe the thought of each other
Frozen in time
Genuine smiles
And laughs exchanged

CHELSEA DEVRIES

The closest thing we will
Ever hold
to being sublime.

PIECE OF MY HEART

I am pretty sure

You hate me
And
All the poems
I write about you.

You probably think
I'm high

High off the scent of
The salt
On my wounds

We were over too soon

And I'm still standing
Looking at the wreckage

Of the mess we made
Or maybe it was just me

Being too naïve
To realize
You were

Out of my league.

HEMOPHILIA

A friend once told me:
"Love isn't a Taylor Swift
music video."

The story of us
May look like a tragedy now
But we don't have bad blood
Between us.

It's not your fault;
You had no clue.

That by cutting me out of your life;
My blood was bad.

The wound you left me with
Has failed to heal
Because
My blood won't clot.

And all the blood loss
Had me lightheaded
Dizzy in love
with how I saw you.

Blinded by your heroic
Light
Unable
To

See
Taste
Smell

The irony
Of your
Lack
Of personal interest
In loving me.

The dark truth
The same color
As dried blood.

You would
Rather
Watch me
Bleed out
Than ever

Be with me.

NO CONTACT ; NO CLOSURE

I just want to cry
Again here I go
With the lies.

I keep on crying
Because
I don't understand
How a man
I put my faith
Trust
And
Love into

Just turned around and said we were never friends.

You couldn't just say
Why
I had to fly the rest of the way solo.

You aren't to blame for my heartache
But you are to blame
For the fact that I may never
Venture
Outside my own comfort zone again.

I will forever look up at the sky
And wonder why I let myself
Fall for you

In the first place.

If all you ever did
In the end
Was go in grace
Save face.
Find a furnishing fixture
For my permanent place.

I don't hate you but I hate that
In the end
It was you
Holding the gun.
The silence between us
Resounds
One single
Still small voice:

Girl, don't fret or sweat.
You only made the wrong choice.

FEELINGS ARE FICKLE

"Once a writer falls in love with you, you will never die."
Sometimes
I think about you.
That's a lie.
I always think about you
And the way I looked
In your eyes.

Like a supernova
Like a celebrity
Like I was incredibly rare
If a heart loves you,
Won't they always love you?

You looked at me like that
Because
Deep inside
I know you cared.

I must just be grateful
For what we shared
Because for me
It was
The closest thing
To fame and fortune
I may ever get.

REQUIEM MASS

I composed a requiem mass
For us
On my birthday.

I wore black
Visited rabbit holes
That turned
Black
With poignancy.

When they realized their chances
Of how the chords of piano keys
Mimicked that laugh

How the sight of your face
Made me remember
That even if both of us
Wanted it
At some point.

We dug an early grave.

This time we couldn't save
The possibility of us
From such a dire
Tragic
Complicated
Confusing

Melancholy
Fate.

With such a cacophonous symphony
I bet even Mozart
Was rolling in his
Grave.

ANTI-SOCIAL MEDIA

Some days on Facebook
I feel so neglected.

My most engaged post?
My new haircut.

Posts about my book or my business?
Snubbed by the shallow waters
of society's idea
that I'm nothing
more than a pretty face.

I'm so social
Horny for friendship.

Yet, in one post,

I'm so lonely.

DEAD POETS SOCIETY

Too many people
Play me
Like a goddamn
Fiddle.

Treat me like I'm little
Or
Of little importance to them.

Only when they need something
Do they slither into
My DMs.

Save your face
For your children
And let's quit
This game of pretend.

You're not a friend
Just a fake.
I never asked for a pet snake.

I don't even understand why I started talking to you
In the first place.

Mouse traps are cheesy.
I'm not here for people pleasin'
Appeasing you

And your self interest.

Honestly
You told me I could message you anytime
And
Then it was you who stopped replying.

BACKWARDS WORLD

I don't like asking people for things

Buy my book
Support my business
Buy the merch; support the cause.

It gathers plenty of eyes and ears
But not much applause.

It's always made me aware
That I'm the underdog.

I recently made a GoFundme
For my parents who
Desperately need a roof.
It wasn't foolproof.
I watched as it sat for months
With no donations
But got plenty of feedback
Questioning
Why I deserve this money.

On the flip side
Some poet I used to
Talk to
Made a Gofundme
Due to needing her breast implants
Removed

Apparently, the toxins
Were making her sick.

She raised $1200 in one hour.

Now you can see why I am sour.

She made a choice to fill her body with
Substances that she had to sign for
Acknowledging the risks.

My parents are getting older
And if their roof caves in
Oh well
That's life.

I'm nobody's wife
But toxicity from society
Makes me nauseous.

This world is backwards
If you're kind
You are labeled too nice.

If you're different looking
Or you think different,
They call you misunderstood.

Bad people portrayed as good
While the good
Watch freedoms fought long and hard for
Be taken away
One by one.

You can't say Jesus
Without giving
Someone the heebie jeebies.

Every word from their mouth
Is made to please.

But please
Help me understand

What a human has to do
To get a little help
Around here.

I'm not asking for much
Just a woman or a man to stand up
For what's right.

Not fight me because I don't agree.
With you
Or
Your ideologies.

Last I checked

Jesus said
All you need
In this life
Was a mustard seed
Sized ounce of faith.

Call me what you will
Classify me as you perceive

But there is no greater law
Than reaping what you sow.
So know what you want
And
Believe in it with all your might.

Fight for what's right.

And if someone needs
A new roof
Consider compassion
Instead of harassing someone
With questions.

Human to human,
At the end of the day
We are all in need of

Love,
Hope,
And
Connection.

WEDDING BAND

I can't understand
Why
I can't
Get a man.

Not necessarily get a man
But keep his interest for more than
A day
A week
A month
A year.

My friend met a guy in August of last year
And she changed her last name on Facebook today.

Me?
I've never been kissed.
Only missed, dissed, and not even taken on a proper date.

Is it because I can't drive?
Yet, I get told I drive guys wild all the time.
It is because I don't put out
Right off the bat?
Home runs aren't free
You know.

What the heck
Do I have to do

To be wined, dined,
Touched and caressed
Like fine silk
Body like milk.

Instead I get turned around
Dizzy
With all the stop and go
Even ghosting
I get from men.

It's sad because all I've ever wanted is to
Fall in love with a man
Who is my forever
My buoy
My boo
My best friend.

CRYING MYSELF TO SLEEP

I'm not alone here.

I'm not the only person
In this cold dark world

That cared too much
Didn't say enough
Fell in love
Too fast

Watched their heart
Shatter like glass
Inside the incubator
In their chest
When the person
We want to talk to most
Won't reach out or text back

But why
Am I always told

Everything you do is wrong.

You don't love right sweetie.
You get obsessed.

You need to stick out this job.
You can't quit a job without a job.

You may know all the rules of the road
But I would feel unsafe with you
Behind the wheel.

You don't need to go to prom.
You need a date.

Save yourself for marriage.
It's better to wait.

It's not what you said;
It's always how you say it
That truly tells
someone
how you really feel.

I'M SCARED

Of what life will be like without my parents
Of losing dogs
Of loving again.

Of never finding a job again
Of my publicity firm going under
Of my roof caving in
Of losing either of my sisters in a tragic accident.

Of flying
Of heights
Of texting him again
Of letting go
Of holding on too long.

Of new places
Of new faces
Of staying the same
Of never growing or learning
Knowing the difference
Of when to walk away or stay.

Of running into you.
Because all the blood would rush to my cheeks
And even if it was dark.
My feelings would come out like steam out
Of a tea kettle.
Airy, breathy, whistling your name

And I'd have to admit
That even though you tried
Everything to push me
Away

Our souls are knit together
With invisible thread

Always
With you
I'm all heart
Over head.

Please say something
I plead with my eyes.

Nice to see you.
You say as you walk away.

And I'm left all alone
With so much still left unsaid.

UNCONVENTIONAL

I've never really believed
I would wed
Or marry

Simply because
What I saw growing up
Was the reality of marriage.

How one person
Lays down
The other carries the cup
And they must carry it
Around like a burden of ash
And urn of all their sacrifice
Burned up.

It's not like the movies
Nothing groovy about it
Sure, the wedding is a fairytale
The booze stays flowing

But nothing prepares you

For what happens after
You jump from job to job
To stay afloat
While your wife goes
Into labor

Prematurely.

The baby remains in the hospital
For a month
Too early
Her little body
The size of
A twelve oz.
Coke can.

Incubating and debating whether
To stay or go
I fought for my life from the get-go.

So please don't tell me
That I must marry
To be someone in this
Mad world

Because I won't believe you.
After all,
I'm unconventional.

For me,
All I've seen
Is that love
Doesn't stay

You only watch it go.

Inspired by Lonely People by Demi Lovato
"All that love is is a means to an end."

TAROT READING

Today,
My favorite psychic
Told me once again
That you were my twin flame.

Yet,
I felt at peace
Because it was clear

She felt you when she read
That you were afraid of what I would say
When you shared your true feelings for me.

I love you still
And
Whether or not you will ever explain

Why you and I stopped the rain from falling
But couldn't stop this fallout
From hurting me and you.

I pray you are ok.

I am done with the games.

WALTZING IN MEMORY

I still look for you
In every face I see
As if my heart can't face
The thought
Of you being ok without me.

It's funny
because
I have days
When the thought of you
Is at a low hum
Like white noise
While I sleep.

Other days
I can't walk
Two steps
In any direction
Without
This pounding
Club soundtrack
Of you
Stuck in my head.

I really hate this.
My life has enough noise.

If I'm honest,

I like that you brightened
Up
The hues
Of the synapses
That fire
In response
To your name.

Saddest of all thoughts:
You don't experience
This same
"Night at the Roxbury"
For me
At all,
Any time, any day.

I think if you did
You would reach out
Or
Try again.

And I wouldn't be moving
In three-fourth time
To the music of you
That plays on and on
Inside of my head
My heart,
My veins.

The music we make
together
more harmonious
Than anything

we sing
into the dark
Apart.

Still,
One single spotlight
I will leave on
In hopes
that I don't
Have to keep spinning circles
Around this fantasy of you,
And I can wrap my arms
Around
The reality of
Your truth
The good, the bad, the ugly,
Every single piece of
What makes you

YOU.

UP IN THE 5D

I dreamt of you last night
And everything was weird
You were there
So was my dog Cooper

We rode a spaceship
And
Every time you came over
To talk to me
You would laugh
That same laugh.

And that's how I knew
You were thinking of me too.

Because the laugh gave me peace
I no longer felt blue.

Dedicated to Cooper who makes me laugh so hard and smiles when he looks at me, and reminds me above all, you must risk it for the biscuit.

TWIN FLAME

Twin flame

You ran
Because you cared too much.

And it scared you.

Yet,
Our candle wick
Still
Sends me a smoke signal
Every now and then.

11:11
The portal is open
I am manifesting
Our union daily.

Praying for your soul
To know true peace
Until that peace mirrors mine

Reminiscing
Our conversations
And
How we finished each other's sentences.

You can't convince me
That isn't some fated destiny romance
Written in the stars.

Until we align again.

WHEEL OF FORTUNE

The pain comes in cycles
First it wrenches and distorts.
Then it trickles back in like a stubborn
Leaky pipe.

Nothing makes sense
And I don't know how to mend this.

I'm no longer broken and bruised
I'm mostly numb and used to the pain.

And I seem unable to gain
From this lesson.

That people leave without explanation
And no words will ever fix you.

You just choose to keep on keeping on.

THE PATH OF THE EMPATH

The path of the empath
Is led by Spirit.

But it's far from bricks paved with gold.

You are told
That you're different
That you're too much
Too intense

All because you came to mend the frayed edges
Of their weary soul.

Healing and helping is your only goal.

Helping rise up a new generation
Of curse breakers
Light workers
Freedom fighters
Both young and old.

Yet, you were never told
When you absorb every energy and emotion

You will mostly feel alone.

NARCISSISTS AND TOXICITY

Sometimes I wonder
What was it about me
That made you target me

I know for one
We are definitely
Wired
Differently.

I refuse to break hearts
Bruise egos
Knowingly.

I've been told
That stepping on people
In order to reach
The top shelf
Or
To feel better about oneself
Is unbecoming.

I don't want to become you
You took every shortcut in the book.
Allowed the bruise, the scar, the wound,
To fester
Instead of heal.

You have no peace inside you

You became my Achilles heel.

I wonder
Was it my dimples
Sunshine hair
Or how positivity leaks out of me
Like a sunbeam peeled off a Sun-in bottle.

I only want to settle this.
What was it about me
That triggered
This hateful
Envious
Jealous response
Inside you?

As if you know anything about me.
I've seen things I wish I hadn't
Heard things that turned my gut
Like a wet rag rung out to dry.
I no longer cry.
I just wonder.

Do you feel better now that I'm no longer
Around to shower you
With kindness, gifts of appreciation,
My words,
My listening ear?

I wonder if you finally found the strength
Within you
To forgive the person
Who made you like this

CHELSEA DEVRIES

Your own Achilles heel.

Most of all
I wonder
If you ever will let yourself heal.

DREAD

Cold sweat
Panic
All along my brow

A heavy anchor
Weighted
In the pit
Of my stomach.

I can't fathom
What life
Will be like
Without you.

You mean
The world to me
If you were to leave
Due to expiration
Or
Accident.

It would completely undo me.

Dedicated to Bambi Beagle: who Suffered Pyometra, Cushing's Disease, And An Allergic Reaction To Antibiotics
All as the epitome of strength and resilience.

RED HEARTS

The queen of sadness
I was absolutely unsure
Of who I was

The moment I met you.

You were all muscles and madness
I wrote soliloquies of sadness

Unaware the way I affected you.

We traded baggage;
You gave me your madness.
I saw my sadness get to you.

We brought a mirror
To each other's shadows
As twins always do.

Unfortunately for me,
I painted the world red for you.

I had no idea
You were

Color blind.

This time, you ran away.
And me?

My kailedescope eyes have seen
Love and romance is nothing
But

Make believe.

WHITE PICK-UP

The first time I ever watched you
Back your pickup
Into your spot in the lot

I knew you drove me to my knees.

I'd been praying
Weeping
Sobbing

For someone like you.

Just a small town boy with no destination
But what's in his rearview.

Your hands gently caressed the wheel
And I silently wished one day

You would caress my heart the same way.

I also wished you would have taught me
How to be confident behind the wheel
But instead

I'm in your rearview
I'm a pin in the map of your mind.

Sometimes my heart races

When I see a Ford F150
Out of the corner
Of my eye.

The letters on the license plate
Don't match the ones etched
On the memo pad in my mind.
No front Ranch Hand barricade.

Forever is a town we dreamed of driving to
But instead you slammed the brakes
Broke my heart

But still

Every now and then
I miss your handsome face.

We must have been destined to drive
Each other crazy enough
To awaken us
To our higher purpose.

Twinflames are meant for such a journey
As us,

Yours and mine.

KALEIDOSCOPE LOVE

The way I love
Is unlike anyone else.

All heels over head
I want you all to myself.

Yet,
The hard part about that is that my head
Knows it's time to leave pack up and go

I realize that I've gone and dug my heels in.

And that's what love is right?

It digs in.
Plants roots
Like a tree
It bends
Sways
And soars with new heights
Expands
And thrives.

I've not gotten the chance to have that kind of love
Only the kind that blooms like a flower, wilts, then dies.

Darling, my love is a prism of every color
My love is one of a kind.

WENDY'S FOR DESSERT

I would sit at my desk
And wonder about your lips.

Was your kiss plump and juicy
Like a chicken sandwich?

I could taste
The mayo
The mustard
The tomato
The lettuce.

All I wanted was a kiss
To satisfy the pains

Of hunger within.

Lick your lips again.

ALL THE THINGS

I shudder
At the sight of more things
Than I should:

Camouflage hoodies
White F-150s
Crocs
Frosty Straws
Text messages that go unanswered
Whispers on my neck
Gotees
Fishing
Hunting
Bikes
Spiderman movies
Men with dirty hands
Romance in movies and tv shows
Love songs
This small town.

It's funny because I never realized
Until now
You had warned me
You wouldn't be back.

You left the song on repeat.

You had me aware that in most social circles
In the end it's fact.

You are the bad guy.

MANIA

Euphorically
Witnessing
Every
Color
Of
Your
Aura

No one else could see it
But I could.
Yet, they call me the crazy one.

I was just being your friend
Because you looked like you needed one.

I will ride your sunshine riptide into oblivion

It's not your fault
I am the last of the real ones.

Inspired by Mania by Fall Out Boy specifically the song, "Last of the
Real Ones."

CODEPENDENCY

The notice went up,
The hours were cut.

One of the other techs said,
"Mr. Suncoast is looking for a new job."

My eyes instantly began to well up.

And I knew you had your hook in me.
I was wrapped around your finger.

Absolutely enthralled by you.

And even now
These aftershocks of you still linger

I remember the finite details of you

Blueberry muffins
How your nostrils flared when you heard me listening to Justin Bieber
Two weeks later,
You told me you weren't a fan of his.

How I looked out my office window
And I caught you looking back at me from a coach across the lot
Prior to me getting the note that said I wasn't cut out for this job.

How you breathed on the back of my neck
When you whispered,

"Are you hiding it from me in the same place as last time?"

And they said your love was unrequited.

But I find that hard to believe.

After all, the mistress you left me for
Wasn't her

It was them.

You were always tied down but not by her
By that job, that place.

But I'm happy for you finally
Getting your own place.

The funniest part
My heart always knew
You were
Not meant to catch it.

I was sent to you to make you rise
Into the man
You were supposed to be.

Ironic isn't it?
That I'm the one stuck in this codependency.

Like the pole I used to hold on a merry go round in my youth
I keep going around and around
The idea of you.

And honestly,
It feels like I'm in the haunted mansion
Dancing with a ghost
Or one of those
Sky dancers
Spinning like a top
And looking so beautiful
Until they crash land
Back in the same spot.

Stuck here.
In the same place.
With you on my mind.

HOLLOW GROUND

When things ended,
People whispered and said
So many things to me:

He didn't deserve you.

You will find someone better.

He sounds like a piece of work.

Yet they were perfectly
Valid things to say
To someone
Who finds
Themselves
Blocked.

Yet would I dare say that about someone
They loved? Absolutely not.
The thought of being that cutting and curt
Would tie me up in knots.
I was hurt
As much by your deafening silence
And their words.
You didn't deserve the blame.
That my name
My face
My eager smile
Caused you pain

For some reason.
Even though
Our season was over
And our chance for love
Fell
With the last crisp autumn leaf.

A cold winter ensued
Like my heart never knew
But
For me and my abnormalities
They were empty vessels
Like words without vowels
Harsh sounding phonetics

All I wanted was one person
to say

Don't give up.
You are worthy of love
And you don't need anyone to heal.

You only need to realize
You are the prize
And no matter if anyone claims you,
You complete yourself.

So anyone who needs it
Let my voice resound.
You are whole.
You are worthy.
You don't have to mingle
If you're single

Or feel wrong
That no one
You wanted
Chose you.

Choose yourself.

THE SUNSET

Our chapter has closed
The sun has set.

But to me
Our time together
Was simply the best.

I was leaving;
You the nest.

Orange and pink skies
Hues of red
The same color of my cheeks
As you smiled at me.

You, my dear, may not have been the one
But
You were one of the good ones.
Different from all the rest.

And every time I think of you
I pray
And wish you the best.

THINGS I NEVER SAID TO YOU

You are beautiful
You are sexy
Your eyes make my heart come alive
Your smile brings me peace
You should laugh more often
I forgive you
I see good in you.
You are destined for great things no small town can confine.
You drive me wild.
You have infinite potential.
You are too hard on yourself.
You have a euphoric aura.
You're incredible.
I think you can do better in love and in life.

I went to text them to you and got a strange
Notification that read:

Return to sender.

DETACHMENT

I'm no longer stationed with you.
I'm free to roam, to fly, to soar.

And your lack of commitment
Little by little

Serves me less pain
Hurts me no more.

CANCUN

The beach wind blowing on my face
The smell of coconut sunscreen
Rain just passed
I witnessed a real la cucaracha
On his back

My American skin
So white
I'm wearing leggings
At the pool

God has blessed me
With a passport
To true freedom

The water so blue
It makes me think
Of the weight
I placed on you.

And how
I expected you to hold me
Up
As if I was sand sifting through
Your fingers

You scrambled to grasp all
That we could be

But the wind
Pulled me
The other way

Our hourglass
Is empty
Our time
Is up.

But still
The sandpaper love
I knew in my past
Can't hold a sunbeam mid sky

To how soft,
Light brown,
And warm
Your heart
Was toward mine.

Cancun, Mexico May 17, 2021

SIMPLICITY

So many people get carried away by the
Complexities of love.

Hair color,
Eye color,
Stature,
Physique.

Yet, they lose sight of the truth
That love,

True love
Weathers
Many storms
Many grey hairs
And waistlines that expand galore.

True love
Was me
Looking into your kind brown eyes
And feeling a peace
I had never known.

True love was
Why
I fell in love
With you

For the simplicity
Of how you
Were
So complex

My chances
With you were
So far-fetched.

Yet,
You enjoyed getting your hands dirty
And smiled when someone asked for your advice
About bikes

You enjoyed spending hours on the water
In a boat
Fishing

Away from it all.

Hunting
So
You could glorify
The prey
On your walls.

You were such a complex
Emotional enigma
But such a simple man

I never planned
To fall in love
With you.

But against all reasoning
And judgement,

I did.

I simply did.

WHAT I NEED

Peace.
To get away
From the thoughts
That keep me up at night
From people who only see lack
Instead of abundance.

To talk to someone
Who makes me see
Things from a new perspective.
To find medicine that makes me happy
Not numb or dizzy.

To be thankful
For what I have
Like my health
Longevity
Vitality
My youth.
Dogs that show me unconditional love
Like a mini version of God.
To get out of this crummy small town
To move out
To make the right amount of money
To dance
To sing
To laugh
To make real friends.

To be more forgiving
To you
For not understanding me,
But yet always underestimating me.

To myself when I feel like
My life has been one big mistake
And for feeling like a fool
For being this hung up on you.
For you
For your inability
To choose
To love me
To get to know
To reply to my texts and explain
One thing:
If you didn't even want me, why did you put so much effort into making
        me think you did.
What I need is truth, clarity, and love.
No more, no less.
In order to rise above
Everything that weighs me down.
To smile instead of frown
To be silly
Say what I feel exactly when I feel it
To focus on the love I do have in my life.
To remind those in the world
With stardust souls
And unicorn hearts
That it's ok to fall apart
Every now and then.

Just as long as you remember:

It's not about the loss of the game

If you try again, you may win.

Dedicated to Zoey
Who inspires me to
Dust myself off
And get back out there
All with her cute bottom tooth grin.

SELF-CARE

Let's get one thing clear
It took you awhile
To get here.

This didn't happen overnight
Not without a fight
Or
A few slipups along the way.

But the person you think you
Need to say those things to
Doesn't care
Didn't see all that you are
And prefers to create distance
Instead of vulnerability
Between you.

You know what I mean.

You came all this way
And you aren't going to
Let what you didn't get to say
To them
Get in the way
Of who you are now.

Whole
At peace with yourself.

God damn proud.

Give yourself a shroud
Of credit
This took many edits
To get this right

Many inner conflicts
Many dialogues
Many nights
Of tears
On silk
Pillowcases.

Repeat after me:
I no longer
Require
Someone who doesn't
Value me
To validate me.

So go ahead
Draft the text
But delete the number.

Darling
The you
You are
Is no longer
Asunder.

So slumber
In peace;

Live your life.

And don't you ever think
Twice about this.
The cost of this clarity
This place you are in
Was much too expensive.

Don't put us through that.
Begin again.

METAMORPHIC VIEW

Out of the chrysalis
Of all I've been through.

Lately
The energy feels different.

Hope is anew
Like the sunrise
Over the morning dew.

I am smiling again
Laughing just because I can

Finding the beauty in being alive.

Not really concerned in who is a ride or die
Alive for me
Set on fire for me
Or
Waiting for me to die.

No longer focused on quantity.
All I want are quality friends.

Someone who texts you after years
Of not speaking
Asking you how you been
And the strangest thing happens.

You realize what a profundity
Your life
Your words
Things you've done and said

Impacted someone enough
That they remember you once again
At 1 a.m.

And for me
It's the simplicity
In the complexities
Of life's most insignificant bonds
And threads

That makes me realize

Life is meant to be succulent
Opulent
A colorful palette of mistakes
Regrets
Moments that push us back
For one second
To see

The height breadth and width of
The Maker's canvas.

PHOTO: MERCURY RETROGRADE

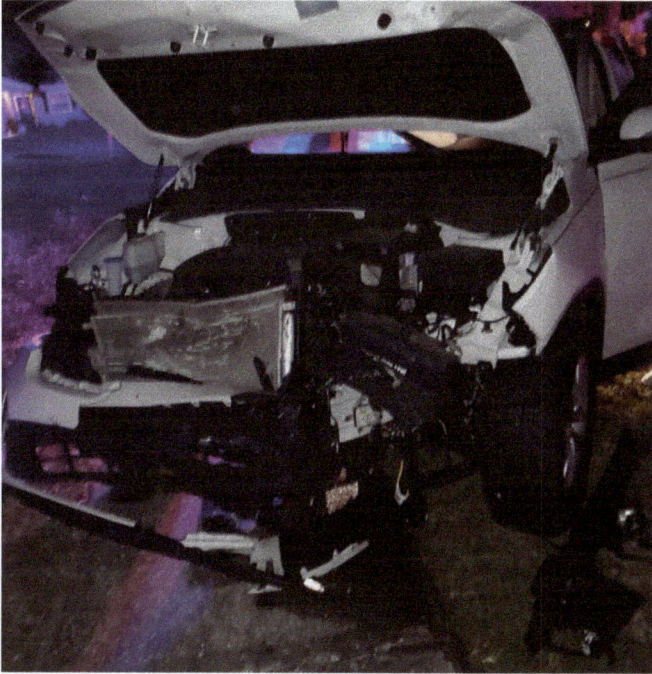

On May 29, 2021 while out on an Ubereats run, some guy ran a stop sign between 9:59 p.m. and 10:01 p.m. he hit us while traveling west on Mitchell Ranch Road. My mom's car was totaled, as her hood popped and most of her engine and transmission fell out on Strada Lane. Upon impact, we must have spun because Mom and I lost consciousness for about a minute or so, and only remember the car landing on the grass and the air bags deploying and filling the car up with smoke. Below is my poem that shares the story of the night we both walked away from this unexpected and devastating incident alive.

MIRACLE ON MITCHELL RANCH

On the first night
Of the Mercury Retrograde
Eveything went dark
There was no sparks
As the car spun out of control

Air bags deployed
Smoke explode
God's hand
Was with me
And mom
As we stepped out of the car

The engine had fallen on the road
Near the stop sign of Strada Lane
Yet God sent an angel
To guide us away
From all we knew before:
Mindlessly numb
Surviving on nothing more
than blue collar bread crumbs.

The angel's name
Santiago
Which is Spanish for
Sanctus
Which means
Saint.
333 appeared

To my mom
And God confirmed
He still had purpose
For our existence;
Our refuge and safe place.

It was a miracle we walked out of the car alive
A miracle occurred in the midst
Of tragedy
On that first night
Of
Mercury Retrograde.

To me
God used what the devil
Meant for harm
To show the world
What it means to be saved.

As I stood
On the scene
Adrenaline
Fueling
My every whim
You were the only person
I wanted to contact
In the heat of the night.

We were bruised and battered
No burns on our skin
But
You were my ICE
Salve for the wounds
Of the chaos within.

NAKED TRUTH

I thought I was over you
But Hell
I taste the truth
And it burns
A little going down

Like a shot of Jose Cuervo.

I wish we would have been given
More of a chance
Because you are all
I ever
Tried to live without
Never understood
That I would crave you
Two years later.

We were almost lovers
But I was almost over you
Then
I got naked with the truth.

Needless to say
I don't enjoy gossip
Or small talk.

It triggered me
To file away

All the hot breath
No sense
Things
They said

Aimed for the boy who stole my heart
On the second day.

Body shaming
Empty comments;
A Wendy's frosty;
All ice no cream.

Me?
I usually stop drop and roll
When the fires of love
Get all over me.

I've always believed
No one was ever good enough
To be with me.

They only wanted
To play
With the fire
Between my thighs.

They tried to hide it,
Disguise it
With flowery descriptions
And sugar-coated lies
But

Love and lust
Walk together
On a thin line.

Then came this boy
Out of the blue
Something about you
Was unlike
All I ever knew
Or believed
About love
Connections
And me.

I thought I doused your flames
With water
But now I look back
And realized
It must have been kerosene.

Twin flames
Don't die out.

They burn eternally.

Ironic isn't it?
All this fire
And
The smoke still rises

For you.

All I wanted you to see
Is all that I saw in you.

Infinite potential
Being stifled by doubt
And half-truths.

If you loved me at all, please do this one thing:
Realize that only YOU can set you FREE
From all that you are and hope to be.

I'll always see you as the firefighter
I didn't know I would need.
Climbing ladders
Day after day
Putting out the fires
I started.

The unsung hero
Who carried me
Away
From the person
I no longer was.

My flame for you
Will always burn
Bright
And
Blue.

Like
The North star
Reminding me
Which way
Leads home.

IDENTITY

My identity isn't found
In your lack of reply
Comments about my
Wardrobe
Intelligence
Sexual prowess
Or
Lack thereof.

My identity
Isn't found
In my social status
relationship status
Or
Place of employment.

My identity is found
In my enjoyment
In who I am
In whose I am

In the love I give
Without expecting
A return
In the freedom
To make mistakes
And learn
From them

In the kindness I show
grace I offer
forgiveness I breathe.

My identity isn't found in you
Or in comparison to you

My identity is found
In the legacy I choose
To leave.

GOOSE EGG

They tell me
Not to put
All my gold eggs
In one basket.

Yet,
The dynamics of love
Scrambles my brain.

Instead,
Of waiting for a man
To domesticate me.

I'll leave these gold eggs
On stranger's doorsteps.
To avoid a mess;
I'd rather bless.

I'll leave the empty basket
At the state line.

Like an unbridled wild stallion,
I'm running free.
Living for no one

But me.

TIMELINES

Who gave you a God complex
And made you an expert
Of how far I should be

In life.

You should have your first kiss by 12
Lost your virginity by 15
Be married by 25
Legal to drive at 16
Have 3 kids by 30
Bought a house
Served jury duty
By 40.

On the other hand
Then there's me
Became a teenage author at fifteen
Why keep dreaming
When you have the means to achieve it.

I was an extra in a movie
Featured on MTV
All before sixteen
Scouted by *Seventeen Magazine*
Solely for the way my abs
Were cut
In a bikini.

Started my own business at 24.
Designed my own clothes at 25.
Ached to see as many places
As a jet plane could take me.

Still want to buy a house one day.
One for me;
One for my parents.

I'm not proud
That when it comes
To normalcy

It's never been my thing

But I can't apologize

That my timeline
Doesn't fit
Your trajectory.
Time is only a human limitation.
Age is just a number.
Souls were meant

To be free.

WHAT IFS

It came time
For me
To move out

From underneath
The crucifix
Of what ifs
I was letting
Weigh me down.

Turns out when you
Heal properly
And have nothing
To carry around

Except love, light, and truth

You are in the perfect position
To truly know
What it means

To be free.

WHAT I'VE LEARNED

That the hardest pain you will ever experience
Comes from a lover you can't let go of,
From a wound that doesn't close.

That when you know you love them;
It's already too late to turn back.
Falling in love is the world's greatest high
But the world's longest fall
if they don't feel the same.

People let you down and hurt you
Regardless of how long you've known them.
Do what's right and forgive.

Live and let live.

I will always love you
Even if you decide to grow sunflowers
In another's garden.
See the world
While you can.

Make love not war.

Ask for help.
Call a friend
Or five.
And tell each one
How much you love them.

People will douse water on your dreams
Out of fear
Of chasing their own.

Yet what you water and invest in
Will grow
Including yourself.

Embrace the unknown.
Trust the Maker.
He has a plan.

The healing processes
are life-long.

Life is but a breath
breathe it in nice and slow.

Home truly is where the heart is.
Home to me will always be you,
My love.

FOR WHAT IT'S WORTH

I wish I met you first
then you wouldn't have to
Feel this hurt.

Now that you see what I saw
The world revolved around her
You were just a place holder
Until someone greater came along.

And honestly that's so messed up
And wrong

From the moment I met you
Even though it hadn't been long
I saw good in you
I knew you weren't single

Because holy hell
It took everything I had
When you were near me
To keep my hands to myself

I didn't even know how she could keep her hands off you.
Maybe nobody ever said that to you.
Told you how handsome you were.
Called you sexy

But damn here we are

I still think the world of you
And you basically wish I didn't exist.

For what it's worth
I would have stuck it out longer than
Anyone who came before me.
Love stays and fights through the battles
Even when it's wounded and bleeding.

Because you made me feel
So glad to be alive
You saved me when I wanted to die

And yeah writing you poem after poem
Even though you always stop replying
Is pretty shitty for my pride.

I don't care
Because I love you.
You made me feel safe as me
Not some generic version
Of myself
I was 100%
The real me
With you.

No holding back;
My inner child let loose.

And I'm sorry I always reach back out
But it's my way of reminding you

That I am so glad you exist.

They say
You know you love someone
If you want them to be happy
Even if it isn't with you.

And when I met you,
Got to know you,
Opened up to you,
Fell in love with you.

I understood
The profundity
In the truth
That truth.
The truth that is you.

But

For what it's worth
The truth is clear
You steered me in the right direction
You set me free
From unexpressed trauma
And unhealed wounds

Even if you weren't the one
I was made to love
I did
I do
Thank you for being you.

I pray you find who
And what makes you happy

STICKS & STONES

Even if that person, that place
Is millions of miles
Away from me.

FINAL WORD FROM THE AUTHOR

Prior to publishing the first edition of this book, I was in the midst of a long overdue deep dive into the healing journey for my mental health. In October 2020, I was officially diagnosed with Asperger's Syndrome which is an autism spectrum disorder that affects social awareness and emotional and mental health.

I chose to wait until the end to share this with you, my reader, so as not to cloud the lens or perspective you read the book through.

Yet, for me, it explains why certain things specifically with that employer were so hard to process and came across as toxic to me but not to the other people that worked there such as:

- The strong smell of dead rat in the ceiling above my office for the duration of my ten months there and the loud machinery in the shop (Sensory Overload).
- The way the guys would joke in the shop and how sometimes I wondered why everyone was laughing (Demeaning comments are not jokes even if the person they are aimed at laughs).
- The very harsh way the manager and his wife spoke to me when they were dealing with mistakes I made, and how I didn't understand why they had to tell the entire staff before pointing them out to me.
- The boss's wife one day while I was outside taking a personal phone call upon my return to my desk, made a joke that I was using a customer's credit card to online shop and that's why I stepped outside. (Maybe to anyone else that would be funny but I don't steal).
- The lack of privacy in my office which left me to always feel like I needed to "mask" in order to get through the day.

Among many other things that I hope to share in my forthcoming memoir but I hope you go back and re-read the collection with that perspective in mind.

For more on Autism and Asperger's Syndrome, some resources I've found to be inclusive and educational and I recommend you check out:

- The Complete Guide to Asperger's Syndrome by Tony Attwood
- Pretending To Be Normal by Liane Holliday Wiley
- Youtube: Asperger's From The Inside
- Youtube: Olivia Hops
- Youtube: Adam Gittings
- Youtube: Autistic Tyla
- Youtube: Neurodivergent Me

ABOUT THE POEMS

Ogres and Hunchbacks: A poem I wrote to help people with autism and Asperger's feel like it's okay to be different. It incorporates my favorite Disney movie: *Hunchback of Notre Dame.*

Different Drum: A poem I wrote that shares my absolute love and romance with street skateboarding which I've followed since 2004. It's been a muse since I was 12 years old: the people have always accepted me within the community and the athletes make their physics look like poetry in motion, and what other sport better showcases breaking bones but getting back up and trying again just because of the passion you feel. I also tend to get bored watching traditional sports but can spend hours watching skateboard videos and contests.

Caffeine Withdrawal: A poem I wrote about this guy I met while working at the Saint Leo Library who absolutely had me all hot and bothered and weak in the knees but that was the extent of our connection as whenever I tried to talk to him, I couldn't think straight. I was all jitters around him.

Perks of Being a Wallflower: a poem that poured out of me after I watched the movie. Looking back, it was my first attempt to tell the people I knew and loved that I was suffering mentally. It also makes sense that this movie triggered it because of the sexual assault I endured in my youth but had never told anyone about.

Happy Medium: A poem I wrote when I moved back home after college and I truly was struggling with my job search, who I was post-school, and utilizes many themes: dating in your twenties, college being a pyramid scheme, and body dysmorphia.

Social Rejection: My response to the 2016 election. I was being presented a candidate who I was told that represented my values and ideals as a female or a feminist but this was my response to that notion.

Angel in Red: This came to me as a caption for a picture my parents later blew up to be a canvas they hung in their living room to celebrate that I am the first and only member of my family to graduate from college with a Bachelor's Degree.

Out of the Woods: I spent many years idolizing many celebrities but the one this poem was about had lead me on for years and I just finally came to the conclusion in 2017 that this was a one-sided fan club, and I walked away from following them or being a fangirl of them. Ironically, they were the muse for the character in my unreleased NA romance novel, *Kickflip My Heart* but my hope for this poem was that it could be read like a general piece when you feel like you are the only one putting in any effort to the relationship, the project at school, etc. One-sided love stinks like a wildfire burning down the woods.

Fight On, Fighter: A poem I wrote after a hard shift working as a hostess at that restaurant. I was pretty depressed but I knew if I didn't write this poem, I may forfeit the fight.

Blank Canvas: A poem I wrote while working at the toxic employer.

I always felt so out of place there but this particular day, I think it was the day, the boss's son and his fiancé got engaged and the boss's wife kept saying to me, "Make sure you congratulate them." And I felt like I wanted to scream.

Fish Out of Water: A poem I wrote about the days when I would visit Weeki Wachee Springs just to see the mermaid show and dream about what it would be like to be a mermaid.

Someday My Prince Will Come; Overrated: I wrote this April 12, 2019. I remember it being a Friday and I realized that day that my feelings for Mr. Suncoast were as deep as the depths of the water along the coastline of either Florida or California but this was one of those poems where the question was still there: do I dive head long into these waters or do I slowly walk and wade in?

Heavy Heart: A poem I wrote in August 2019 when it felt like Mr. Suncoast and I were destined for nothing more than saving each other from making the same bad choices in love but not meant to be together.

He Can't Love Me: My response to when he first blocked me on Facebook on January 6, 2020. I utilize and repeat words and phrases for emphasis; the same way lyricists do in music because music was our commonality and we both would light up whenever we talked about it while at work.

Unacknowledged: The longest poem I ever wrote in April 2020 at 30 stanzas and 738 words. It poured out of me because I was hung up on this idea that I needed to acknowledge him in my novel when I published it so he would know how I felt about him but this came out and to this day, it's this narrative poem that tells the entire story of what happened there, between us and around us. I utilize themes of the Greatest Showman movie and Tim Burton because that place was dark, dreary, and it smelt like an elephant's trough mostly because there were dead rats in the ceiling the entire duration of my employment there.

SelfLess Love: A poem I wrote after realizing that every person I've ever loved or tried to love has left me feeling like I gave everything I had just so they would see their own potential and all I got was toxicity or heartache in return.

Ghosts Of My Past: This poem was inspired by a daydream I had where I was talking to Mr. Suncoast and saying, "I worked there because I'm always trying to be the light, and lighten the load of those around me." And in the daydream, I saw the orb ball from Disney's Haunted Mansion movie.

Enigmatic Energy: I became very invested in spirituality and the law of attraction as part of my healing process and I found a video on Youtube that teaches you to manifest a text from someone you haven't heard from in a while, and for the life of me, I tried several different times but to no avail…it remains a mystery. Thus, this poem came from that experience.

Fool For You: I wrote this after I shared a stanza on Instagram from Unacknowledged and someone actually commented and said some rude things, and it made me so angry I wrote this poem but it was this poem that made me realize that I didn't just have a set of poems, I had a collection. It's one thing I hate about social media. You post to share but people always comment on my posts acting like I asked for their opinion or suggestion about something. No, I'm very aware of what I have to do, and nothing or no one will stop me. Not even you, anonymous commenter.

Seeking Clarity: Another poem that utilizes concepts from spirituality and the belief in twin flames: two halves of the same soul that get separated upon their descension from heaven.

You Would Never Believe This: This poem is about the idea that you end up getting to talk to or see that person who left your life out of the blue and you get to tell them all the things you've been up to, and you get one last chance to thank them for being in your life even if wasn't for forever.

Heart Versus Mind: Inspired by "The 1" by Taylor Swift, it came to me after listening to *Folklore* non-stop for 3 days straight. I wanted to tell him something about one of the songs but realized he probably didn't want to hear from me anyway. I wrote this poem instead.

Papercuts and Broken Hearts: It felt appropriate to make books and men become a joint metaphor since both make me happy and my heart race.

Asexual Poem: In February 2020, I posted a blog to my website where I shared my sexuality and this poem was a continuation of my sharing that with the world. And I wrote this in a poetry collection so that other people like me who are both asexual and demisexual feel safe to be themselves. It was also my way of "coming out" to my family since I didn't know any other way to do that.

Stop Scrolling; Start Living: a poem inspired by the 2020 pandemic and how I found myself excessively scrolling but for someone with mental health, if you find yourself doing that with the same mindlessness, the people around you should recognize that it's a cry for help, and following writing this: I started walking 3-5 miles a day around my neighborhood in order to "get out" on days when I can't physically change my zip code or can't afford an escape.

What I Meant By Thanks For The Opportunity: During my unemployment testimony with the toxic employer, one thing they actually made a huge deal about was that my resignation letter was two statements: it read thanks for the opportunity. I appreciate all I have learned here. I wrote that because it was a formal way of saying this opportunity was through, but it was the nicest way I could find with saying thanks for teaching me what bad business looks like. I'll be sure to never make mistakes like yours ever again.

Never Enough; Mistake: During the testimony, the boss's wife clear as day said to me, "I think it's important to focus on your mistakes." And I instantly knew I made the right decision leaving there because being around people who focus on flaws, mistakes, and never let you progress are people who will enable you to settle in life.

Ms. Lonely: A poem where I address my lack of a romantic relationship in any serious capacity It's also about not settling in love or in life no matter how "lonely" you feel.

Thoughts While Having a Panic Attack: A poem I wrote after suffering a PTSD panic attack where I felt like I was choking out my feelings for Mr. Suncoast and instead of helping me find my bearings, he turned his back.

What If: a poem I wrote about trying to figure out why I was ghosted. I had many theories including one where I was convinced that they had paid him to flirt with me in order to make fun of me having a crush just so they could watch Mr. Suncoast not choose me. Not proud of that one but when someone works for an at-will employer, the employees that remain can be threatened they will lose their job if they talk to a former employee, and that's probably what really happened because outside of

Mr. Suncoast, I reached out to one of the other guys that still works there and also got no response by both text and social media.

Piece of My Heart: This one came to me while out for one of my long walks, I kept seeing a scene of a car accident and it occurred to me the longer I focused on this, the longer I was standing at the scene looking at the tragedy instead of living my life and making new memories.

Hemophilia: I kept thinking of Taylor Swift's song *Bad Blood* and realized that I must have bad blood because I can't seem to close this wound, every time I thought I was ok, it would bleed another poem out of me, and that was the idea behind this one but it also brings awareness to this rare but real medical condition.

Feelings are Fickle: I remember this one was written while I was at work, I was sitting in the backseat of my mom's car, and it became this piece about how you can truly never forget the way someone looks at you when they care about you, no matter if they admit it or not.

Requiem Mass: My 29th birthday was one of the saddest I ever had in a long time. Sure, I celebrated by staying in and watching my favorite movies, but I wished the entire day to hear from him, or for there to be some sign that he was going to come back. I did get the idea for this one after watching *Amadeus* starring Tom Hulce who actually is the voice of Quasimodo in Disney's *Hunchback of Notre Dame*. It came to me near the end of the film when they toss Mozart's body in an unmarked grave, and it was that image that stuck with me and one of Mozart's last compositions was his Requiem Mass. What a morbid way for a genius such as him to go.

Anti-Social Media: After releasing my book, I thought I would instantly become more popular on social media. Not sure where the thought came from but this poem came to me after I noticed my posts weren't getting the engagement they deserved and the only one that did was a picture of my new haircut. It was this post that later made me do some serious cleansing of my social media, and eventually delete my old Instagram, and my Twitter page despite having nearly 5000 followers there. From a marketing perspective, the social media that flourishes is the one you are consistent with, and show up for. You also have to know when some avenues of strategy are dead, and when other avenues are blooming. Always Go where the wild things are. The networks that make you feel like you are truly connected are the ones worth keeping, everything else isn't worth your mental health.

Dead Poets Society: This is one of two poems I wrote about a poet (or poets) I befriended prior to releasing my book who I ended up having to block on everything because their friendship was entirely one-sided and I was starting to learn the practice of placing boundaries in place when something didn't feel right for me personally. They didn't take it well.

Backwords World: This was based on those poets again and one of them really did make a GoFundMe to raise money for her toxin sickness. The reason it bothered me is because prior to announcing this page, and her illness, she announced herself as a best-selling poet and even held a giveaway on her Tiktok where she announced me as the winner in front of over 45K followers where she gave out a $100 VISA giftcard, candles and a free copy of her poetry collection. I never received my prize and realized that I had been set up once again, so I knew that I had to leave the connections as quietly as I could while still ensuring I was at peace overall. This also all happened right after I found out I had Asperger's and basically had a hard time accepting that diagnosis, and how it hadn't been found out or realized by anyone beside my youngest sister until I was 29 years young. I basically felt like I didn't know how to relate to anyone after getting the diagnosis and as I shared on my website in a blog, the doctor who gave me the evaluation made me very self-conscious because he made a huge deal about me not having a boyfriend, and never having a serious one which triggered me because of the toxic employer and how it felt like all they cared about me was my relationship status. My work performance, my dedication to be a better employee, they were all null and void because I was single.

Wedding Band: This was inspired by a friend who changed her name on Facebook without telling me she'd even gotten engaged and my response to it.

Crying Myself To Sleep: A poem I wrote while actually crying myself to sleep after someone I care about said something that truly hurt me, and I thought of all the highly sensitive people in the world who feel unable to process the hurt from the way people say things not entirely what they said.

I'm Scared: This was written while having an anxiety attack about all of life's what ifs.

Unconventional: This was written about my own parents and how I've always felt pessimistic when I thought about marrying someone or even thinking someone would promise me forever even if not through marriage.

Tarot Reading: I spent a lot of money on Tarot readings in order to find some answers after leaving that employer but this particular one was one of the last I did. Tarot readings are actually cheaper than counseling and they act as mediators for people who are struggling with something in their life. Overall, all the tarot readings confirmed many inner knowings I felt while working there, and after leaving there.

Waltzing in Memory: This was written while I was getting my hair done at Ulta Beauty but it was this cool music based metaphor about dancing with the memory of someone, and since music was our commonality, it was another one inspired by Mr.Suncoast.

Up in the 5D: Based on a real dream I had and in spirituality, they say that when you dream of someone it's you connecting with their soul in the fifth dimension which is only accessible through your subconscious mind.

Wheel of Fortune: Based on the tarot card that represents the cycle of life, how it flows with good and bad. It incorporates this idea of destiny and how nobody can avoid what's predestined for each of us: the people we meet, the opportunities that present themselves, the creative ideas that find their way into our frontal lobe, even the tragedies we suffer. They are all interconnected. The card also serves as a reminder that if a cycle has ended in your life, what lesson did you learn from it.

The Path of The Empath: I wrote this prior to finding out I was autistic but I still believe I am an empath because I can feel energies in a room, even those who aren't visible or aren't expressed. It can be overwhelming and it was one thing that I came to really understand about myself while working at that employer.

Narcissists and Toxicity: A poem written to a person who hurt you so brutally but it's after much time has past and you wonder if they have found healing the way you have. It's a poem that showcases the idea that you can either become bitter or better when someone hurts you, and especially after suffering trauma.

Dread: My dog Hazel was actually showcasing many symptoms of being near-death and this poem was my response to the idea of losing her so soon after her Cushings diagnosis.

Red Hearts: I just kept picturing those cards in the Disney version of *Alice in Wonderland* who paint the flowers red and I kept hearing, "Off with her head." It was also inspired by the image of Alice shrinking herself into that little glass bottle and floating on an ocean of her own tears.

White Pick-up: A poem I wrote after seeing how many white pick-ups around my city but knowing none of them were him because his truck is very distinct. Coincidentally, on July 10, 2021, he ended up driving next to my mom up Little Road, and the only way I realized it was him was because my mom said he had been tailgating her so I looked up and saw his white truck next to us, and it was him because the license plate matched. And by the time I was going to roll the window down and scream his name, he sped up and got ahead of us, and I waved at him as he headed up the road. A week later on July 17, 2021 at around the same time as the week prior, I was out running errands and saw his truck in the left turn lane and he was going to the Verizon store near me with his sister and mom. It was a very strange thing but God truly has a great sense of humor and God did tell me he was bringing him back. I just never thought it would be in such a big way but he does things beyond what we ask or think.

Kaleidescope Love: A poem about the many colors of love and how if your love is intense, they tell you to water it down but I say go big or go home.

Wendy's For Dessert: A food metaphor based on Mr.Suncoast's lunch about how sometimes you can be hungry but not for food.

All the Things: A list of things I started to roll my eyes over whenever I saw them in real life when I started to think he wouldn't come back.

Mania: Inspired by how I dedicate the song, "The Last of The Real Ones," to Mr.Suncoast but also shows how much I enjoyed this album by Fall Out Boy.

Codependency: A cool poem where I examine all the things he did, and how I really did get sad when someone said he may get a new job, I even told my mom and she made a funny comment that if he left, that place would seize to exist.

Hollow Ground: A poem about how harmful the things people say to you post breakup can be, and how nothing except going inward and working on loving yourself are the hollow ground necessary to rebuild your foundation and start again.

The Sunset: A poem I wrote after watching the sunset while out on one of my walks.

Things I Never Said To You: This poem was inspired by all the things I felt like I should have said to him and how instead of saying them to him, I would be better looking in the mirror and saying them to myself.

Detachment: This poem was originally longer but I left the final stanza because it really was the only one I liked from this poem. It's about when you have finally healed and you realize that it's ok to have met someone, and had feelings for them, and for you not to get the happy ending.

Cancun: A poem I wrote while in Cancun Mexico inspired by the sights, smells, and experience of visiting that part of Mexico for the first time.

Simplicity: A poem I wrote during National Poetry Month 2021 about how the simple life gets such a bad rep but honestly it's what we all aspire to in one way or another, and how simply falling in love with a simpleton changed my life forever.

Metamorphic View: A poem I wrote after a person I hadn't heard from in years texted me out of the blue and I spent the entire day texting them but it happened on April Fool's Day 2021 so I really thought at first that it was someone pulling a prank on me pretending to be Mr.Suncoast.

Naked Truth: A truth I came to terms with in Mexico was that tequila really helps you get naked…and well, it also brings up hidden truths. I ended up reading It Ends With Us by Colleen Hoover and it brought up all these emotions where I had to realize I was still hoping he was going to wake up and come back, but at the same time, this poem makes peace with the notion that he may never, and I wanted him to know I saw you, I saw the good in you, and I will always be grateful you existed in my life when you did.

Identity: A poem I wrote after sending him a happy birthday text in 2021 and he saying thank you but once I gave him 3 clues of who it was, he didn't reply but ended up unblocking me on Facebook for the second time.

Goose Egg: A poem I wrote where I was impatient with the lack of romantic love in my life. It plays on the notion of feeling like I've gotten nothing but a big old goose egg in love but that doesn't mean I can't live the rest of my life living and not just being alive.

Timelines: A poem written about something someone said the same day that irked me but made me write this: No one gets to tell you how far you are in life except you. You don't have to follow the same timeline as anyone. I am proof of that. I didn't wait to become a writer. At 15, I knew I wanted to make it my job so I just went for it even though my parents didn't approve. Looking back, it was this tenacity and determination that I try to channel now as an adult when I can't seem to figure out how to even get up out of bed.

What Ifs: A poem I came up with out on one of my walks where I kept hearing what if all those what ifs was a crucifix, would you hand it over and let me carry it for you? And I knew that the only way to stop the what if game was to cast my care on Him who cares for me.

What I've Learned: A poem I wrote following "Naked Truth" where I was entirely happy after getting a thank you from Mr. Suncoast and for realizing that even if it wasn't the happy ending I wanted, God restored that connection and proved to me that what we had shared was something that affected both of us to grow and flourish, and made me grateful for how even the smallest of details matters to God, and he loves us THAT much.

For What It's Worth: A poem I recently wrote where I used this universal truth and finding my way to accepting it

Trauma happens and harms us.
But I often wonder if the second wave—
When your story is misbelieved, mistrusted, and misaligned.

May your story find safe harbor
In the presence of people
Who will honor both
Vulnerability and resilience.
— KJRamseyWrites

What if we were transparent
About our own failures,
Not as some kind of
Performative vulnerability,
But as an invitation
To collectively de-stigmatize
The messy process
Of lifelong learning?
— Raechael Alaia

One day
You will tell your story
Of how you overcame
What you went through
And it will be someone else's
Survival guide
— Bene Brown

"Why are you so nice even to people
who are rude to you?"
"Because, I too, have been rude
To nice people
& I know that rudeness comes from a place of roaring pain.
& Only kindness soothes it."
— By The Word

"Believe, when you are unhappy, that there is something for you to do in the
world. So long as you can sweeten another's pain, life is not in vain."
— Helen Keller

ACKNOWLEDGEMENTS

Jesus: Thank you for all you do, all you've done, and what you still plan to bring to pass in my life. I am so very blessed. You are my vindicator. You are fighting my battles. You definitely gave me beauty for my ashes because as I write this second dedication to you, I feel entirely brand new. Is everything in my life perfect? Absolutely not. Yet, I am so grateful for everything that happened since this book came to be, and everything you lead that day of small beginnings to mean in my life, and subsequently how you used it for so much more than what it appeared at the time. The fog has been removed from the windows in my soul. Jesus, thank you for helping me learn that by loving you, leaning into you on the days when confusion and doubt surround me, I can not and will not fail. Thank you for also helping me heal, and for helping all the people who read this book heal too. You are so very good. I truly know now what it means to live as if I'm alive and my eyes are wide open, the sleeper has been called to rise.

I ask you to do a work in the life of anyone who reads this book: that the words I write meet them in the midst of their suffering, grief, and brokenness and comforts them, and opens their hearts and minds to true healing, your grace finds strength in their weakness, and they are surrounded by a love that is full of compassion, quick to forgive, slow to anger, and has its default setting in kindness.
Thank you for all you do in and through me. I love you, Lord.

Mom: *You are my sunshine, my only sunshine. You make me happy when skies are gray. You'll never know dear how much I love you. Please, don't take my sunshine away.* Thanks for everything and rooting for us still. Thanks for being my partner in crime and for reading this through when I was done

215

to make sure it read cohesively. I don't know where I would be without you in my life. Seriously lady, you are amazing.

Dad: I still laugh every time I read your Goodreads review. You always know how to make me laugh. Thanks for sharing my book with people all over the country when you are on the job. I am so grateful you work as hard as you do. Thanks for teaching me what blue collar work ethic looks like. Love you Pops!

Mr. Suncoast: There is a less than 3% chance you'll read this but if you happen to find this book someday and read it cover to cover, I hope you find the courage to reach out and we can have a real conversation about it. I hope you don't get intimidated that I found a muse within you, and I haven't stopped writing since I met you. I just thought it was important to put it all out there, even my ugly truths because well life is short and the healing process taught me to be unafraid of your scars because they are the marks God uses most to move people. I also just wanted you to have something to remind you that someone showered you with unconditional love, and poetry that reminds you of it, even if we never speak again. I pray for you every day still but I must say, K, I miss your friendship still to this day. I'll never understand why we couldn't stay friends because meeting you changed my entire life. Please be well, stay safe, and make good choices especially in music.

Since this might be the last time I ever write you a poem or say anything to you, I think you should listen to *Somebody Does by Tigerlily*.
It's a song I dedicate to you and to anyone out there working harder than most just to get by. I dedicate it to you because for ten months, it was you who got me up and out of bed showing up to that job. It was you whose face still sticks with me when I am unsure or upset. It provides me peace mostly. My hope for you is still the same: I hope you become somebody great and you are loved by somebody great because to me, you were the greatest turn of events in my life.

Nick Trandahl: Thank you for being one of the best poets I ever be-friended. I feel cool being able to call you my friend. I can't wait to read your next collection. You are sheer brilliance. Never stop writing. And thank you for always cheering me on.

Shaye Baker: Funny how God connects you with the right people right on time. You are such an inspiration to me as a poet and brother in Christ. Thank you for cheering me on. I appreciate you.

My Launch Team: Thank you all for your support, for your belief in the expansion of this book, and for your belief in me as a writer. It is such a gift. You are all such a blessing to me.

My Indian friends and readers: Thank YOU for the tremendous support of this collection in its incubation/first edition phase. When I made that Amazon best-seller list, I really was blown away. I also felt like I was wit-nessing it happen to someone else. Thank you for your love, your encour-aging messages on the hard days, and for the beauty of your culture and country. It inspires me so very much.
To anyone out there who never gets a thank you: Thank YOU for being you, changing, growing, learning, loving, healing, breaking, mending, and inspiring writers like me to witness greatness in the ordinary every day.

Thank you to:

— George Beckman of Beckman editing for making a really raw and ca-thartic prose piece read so much more fluently and yet still allowed to re-tain its beauty and wonder. Thank you for your keen eye and for believing in me and my story.

— Lulu Seldon of Lulu Seldon Photography: Thanks for capturing me in the place that makes my heart sing a joyous hymn. And thank you for being such a genuine person. I look forward to the next time I can come out there to visit.

— My readers: Thanks for loving my art. For riding the waves of my brutal honesty and cathartic soul. And for making me feel that being this brave and vulnerable is cool in some small social circles. Thank you for helping me take the heart of this collection, and water it with love while also nurturing it into what it has blossomed into.

You have reached the end of this collection.
Please leave a review telling me how it resonated on Goodreads,
Amazon, and Barnes and Noble.

And connect with me on my two favorite platforms:
Instagram @onegirlrevolution26_
Youtube youtube.com/ChelseaDeVries

Purchase something magical for your wardrobe or your bookshelf:
www.etsy.com/shop/UnicornPixieDesigns

ABOUT THE AUTHOR

Chelsea DeVries wanted to be a writer since she was seven years old. Her first publishing credit came at the age of 14 with a poem in a student anthology. She then wrote nonstop while doing IB classes in high school. She published two YA novels while still in high school which after ten years she rewrote as an NA romance that she looks to put out as her next publication. She is a seeker of justice and uses her words to free the world's outcasted, peculiar, and underdogs from the chains that bind them. When not writing she runs and does publicity for authors, musicians, and corporate entities with her bookish brand The Smart Cookie Philes. Though she's Florida born and raised, she has New Jersey in her veins. She enjoys living life large: by enjoying big mugs of dark roast, big slices of cheesecake, and spending countless hours standing near big bodies of water. DeVries was diagnosed with Asperger's in October 2020. She currently lives in Port Richey, FL with her squad of three dogs. You can follow her on Instagram at @onegirlrevolution26_ and squad at @dasquad26.

www.ingramcontent.com/pod-product-compliance
Lightning Source LLC
Chambersburg PA
CBHW071853090426
42811CB00004B/592